10 - 18

LADDER
shifts

LADDER *shifts*

NEW REALITIES | RAPID CHANGE | YOUR DESTINY

SAMUEL R. CHAND

Printed in the United States of America

Published by:
Mall Publishing Company
12693 Cold Springs Drive
Huntley, Illinois 60142
Toll Free: 1-877-203-2453
E-mail: info@mallpublishing.biz
Website: www.mallpublishing.biz

Layout by Marlon B. Villadiego

ISBN 0-9777273-7-8

Scripture references are from the following versions:

KJV: King James Version.

MSG: Scripture quotations from THE MESSAGE. Copyright © by Eugene H. Peterson 1993, 1994, 1995, 1996, 2000, 2001, 2002. Used by permission of NavPress Publishing Group.

NIV: Scripture quotations are taken from the Holy Bible, New International Version®. NIV®. Copyright © 1973, 1978, 1984 by International Bible Society. Used by permission of Zondervan. All rights reserved.

For licensing / copyright information, for additional copies or for use in specialized settings contact:

info@samchand.com

Acknowledgements

You never make LadderShifts by yourself. My wife Brenda has helped me at each shift. Thank you Brenda for being my best ladder holder. Thanks for believing in me.

A special note of appreciation to my ghostwriter, Pat Russo, who took all my raw thinking, notes, interviews and often ambiguous concepts and produced this organized book.

Other Books by Samuel R. Chand

Failure: The Womb of Success

Futuring: Leading Your Church into Tomorrow

Who's Holding Your Ladder?

Who Moved Your Ladder?

What's Shakin' Your Ladder?

For additional resources, see the back of this book.

www.samchand.com

Table of Contents

The Ladder Story

Waiting for someone to call me into the sanctuary, I stared out the window. As I meditated on the points I wanted to cover as a featured speaker at this conference, something in the street below caught my attention.

A man stood on a ladder painting—not that uncommon a sight. I smiled, remembering my student days in Bible college. I had spent my summers doing that kind of work. Yet I couldn't take my eyes off the man. For several minutes, I watched his graceful motions as he moved his brush and roller across the surface.

As I watched, I noticed that this painter was only covering a limited area. He stretched as far as he could to the left, to the right and even reached above his head. It also occurred to me that he was only going to the height that he was comfortable at, even though the extension ladder he was using could reach much higher.

From my painting experience, I remembered that once I was on the ladder and had the necessary resources, I painted a much larger area before taking the additional time needed to climb down and relocate the ladder. It was an efficient method.

"Why isn't he going higher to paint all the way up? What would allow him to go higher?" I asked myself. Then I saw the reason—no one was holding his ladder. By himself, the painter couldn't go any further. He had done everything he could by himself. He needed help.

As I watched his graceful strokes, I realized the leadership parallels. Whether we're talking about churches, businesses or non-profit organizations, the effectiveness of a leader depends on the person or persons holding the ladder—those who are in support roles.

The height that a visionary leader reaches on the ladder to their vision is not controlled by the leader's capabilities. It's not even controlled by how inspiring their vision might be. It's controlled by who's holding the ladder.

Then another thought struck me: Those who hold the ladders are as important as the leaders themselves.

The visionaries could have all the training possible, the most expensive equipment, years of experience and knowledge about painting, and a blend of expertise and passion about their craft. But that's not the deciding factor. The ladder holder determines the height to which the ladder climber ascends. "That's it!" I cried aloud. "Those who hold the ladder control the ascent of the visionaries."

Additionally, a ladder holder who may be very capable with a 20-foot extension ladder (or vision) may not be the person you want holding your 45-foot extension ladder (a new or enlarged vision). Old ladder holders are rarely adequate at holding new ladders.

My book, *Who's Holding Your Ladder?*, explains this powerful concept. It explains the need for qualified ladder holders and the necessary qualifications, differentiates between leaders and managers, and describes how you can turn your ladder holders into ladder climbers.

For other *Ladder* books and information, visit www.samchand.com

Introduction

Y our heart beats to the rhythm of your destiny.

It's the song that fills your life and the vision that compels you forward.

It's your destiny that gives purpose to your steps.

Everyone has a destiny, but not everyone walks the path to fulfilling it. If you're reading this book, it's likely that you're already taking steps to reach your destiny, to climb the ladder that's before you. In the chapters that follow, I hope to help you to more fully embrace your destiny by shedding light on the seven new rungs that all leaders climb on their ladder to destiny.

Regardless of your level of leadership, all leaders deal with the same basic issues. It doesn't matter whether you have a limited or an extensive leadership background, or whether your vision is for a business, a church, or a non-profit organization. The CEO of Yahoo, the pastor of a small church, and the person running a non-profit organization are all concerned with two major issues:

- Walking the seven steps toward your destiny

- Dealing with the eight challenges you face along the way

Reaching Your Destiny

The journey that leads to your destiny consists of seven sequential steps. Each step is necessary; there can be no shortcuts to this process. Reaching your destiny requires taking each of the following steps in the corresponding order:

1. Thoughts
2. Words
3. Decisions
4. Actions

5. Habits
6. Character
7. Destiny

1. **Thoughts.** Everything that you see in the world – except for what grows naturally – begins as a thought. Our light fixtures, our cars, the chair you're sitting on, the book that you're reading began as thoughts. When the Bible says, "As a man thinks in his heart, so is he[1]," it's telling us that our thoughts help to shape our destiny. Everything begins with a thought. These thoughts are expressed in what we say.

2. **Words.** Typically, we verbalize our thoughts about our destiny by saying things like, "I wonder what it would be like…" It's not hard to imagine Wilbur Wright saying, "I wonder what it

would be like if we could fly." It's easy to imagine Henry Ford saying, "I wonder what it would be like if we could mass-produce cars" or for Thomas Edison to express his thoughts about the light bulb. The Bible's book of Genesis tells us that this is a Scriptural pattern. It was the *word* of God that created what we now see around us. Everything began as a thought in God's mind, which led to these words, "Let us make man in our image[2]."

3. **Decisions.** Once you've spoken the words, they lead to decisions that coincide with your words. You might tell someone, "This is what I'm going to do." Those decisions lead to certain actions.

4. **Actions.** People tend to believe that they can *start* their journey by taking action. For example, if they want to lose 20 pounds, they immediately start by doing something about it. Unfortunately, jumping into behavior modification is not the appropriate starting place. That's why statistics show that 80 percent of people who lose weight gain it all back. It's because actions without strong underlying thoughts, words and decisions don't provide the necessary foundation for success.

The place to start is with your *thoughts*. You have to know what being overweight is doing for you and consider how it's hurting you. Then you start telling yourself, your family, and your friends, "I need to lose weight. I think I'm going to go on a diet and start exercising." Then you make decisions about what changes you're going to make in the foods you eat and what exercises you'll do. There's nothing wrong with taking action, but you cannot ignore the three previous steps if you want to be successful.

5. **Habits.** When you continue an action long enough, it becomes a habit. We all know people who are habitually late. It's not an occasional thing; they do it all the time. It comes from lazy thinking and talking, a lack of good decisions and inadequate actions. All of these foundational behaviors are important because they create habits. And it's your habits that create your character.

6. **Character.** Our character is the sum of our habits. When Aristotle wrote, "We are what we repeatedly do," he made it clear that there's a direct connection between who we are and what we do. He underscored this fact by concluding, "Excellence, then, is not an act, but a habit." A habit that's performed long enough becomes part of your character. If you know someone who is habitually late, you know that it's hard to expect different behavior from him or her. Their habit has become part of who they are and it has shaped their character.

7. **Destiny.** Eventually, your character will lead you to your destiny. There are no shortcuts to success, no easy roads to get there. Everybody wants to have their destiny fulfilled, but not everyone wants to walk through the entire process. But that is what's required.

Realizing your destiny requires deliberate thought and action. You have to continually watch your thoughts because whatever you obsess about is what you'll bring about. You must follow the appropriate path and organize yourself adequately. Everything you think, say and do must be congruent with your destiny. If it isn't, you won't end up in the place you want to go.

These consecutive steps — from your thoughts to your character — are the new rungs that all leaders climb on their ladder to destiny. Now that you're aware of how these seemingly inconsequential steps can help you reach your destiny, your chances of fulfillment are already greatly advanced.

Dealing with New Challenges

In addition to following the right path, reaching your destiny also requires that you deal appropriately with many bewildering issues and uncomfortable circumstances.

You have to chart your course through unfamiliar territory, address issues for which your perspective seems inadequate, and experience pains that no college or training program could have adequately anticipated. You have to diplomatically sort out what you need from the people supporting you, ensure that you're giving sufficient time to the appropriate priorities, and deal with circumstances that you hadn't planned on and for which you might not be prepared. And you'll have to do it all without losing the passion that fires you or your openness to the sudden inspiration of new possibilities.

These are the predominant themes that are being faced by nearly all of the leaders that I work with. Every leader – whether you're running Microsoft, Google, or the church down the street – is dealing with these issues. You may not be experiencing all seven of them, but most of us are dealing with three at any given time. Because life is dynamic, we may experience one to a lesser degree today, while one that hadn't affected us will suddenly register off the scale tomorrow.

Watch any leader of any significance and you'll see them dealing with these eight issues:

- New Places
- New Perspective
- New People
- New Pains
- New Priorities
- New Preparation
- New Passion
- New Possibilities

Putting politics aside, we can observe President George W. Bush facing each of them:

- He has been taken to new **places** in his career because of 9-11, the effects of multiple hurricanes, as well as the economy and rising oil prices.

- In terms of **perspective**, he's had to evaluate many issues and problems at a higher level than the ones on which they were created.

- He's needed **people** around him that can give him sound recommendations.

- He certainly has had new **pains**, such as the setback with nominating a new Supreme Court justice.

- He started off his second term with a strong Social Security issue. Then his **priorities** had to change.

- When Hurricane Rita was coming in right after Hurricane Katrina, he had to quickly scuttle his planning and **prepare** to mobilize wherever it hit, since he didn't know where that would be.

- His **passion** for certain issues has probably changed just because of the daily challenges he's facing.

- Overall, it's his openness to new **possibilities** that ultimately determines his destiny and his legacy.

I've seen these eight issues unfolding when I work with pastors, organizations, and business leaders. Each situation and each leader has validated their importance in each situation.

Your biggest challenge isn't money, it isn't your building plans, or your marketing strategies. It's gaining insight into how these eight challenges are affecting you so that you can provide the leadership that's needed in that context. That's what leadership is about. It's about making sense of what's happening in your environment and moving your organization forward. It's about learning and letting others benefit by sharing your perspective. It's about climbing the ladder to your destiny and preparing other leaders for the challenges that they will face on their journey.

1

New People

*My main job was developing talent. I was a gardener providing water
and other nourishment to our top 750 people.
Of course, I had to pull a few weeds, too.*

– Jack Welch, former chairman and CEO, General Electric Corp.

Paul is sweating. His largest client just called, asking for earlier
completion of an important project. Paul's been up nearly all night,
scrambling to meet his regular project deadlines. Despite the success
of his small software company, he finds it increasingly difficult to
retain responsible employees. While there's no shortage of qualified
programmers, their inability to meet deadlines or even to show up for
work has forced him to let a number of them go. His most talented
people are frequently lured away by offers from larger companies.
Staring at the ringing phone, Paul wonders if he can afford to hire
someone to deal with these human-resources challenges.

L eadership is filled with people issues. No leader is immune to
them; they come with the territory. Like Paul, maybe you find
yourself in need of some new people in your life. Perhaps you're
wondering why you're not getting the support you need from people

who have always been helpful in the past. Maybe you wish you could find someone to simply validate the challenges that you're dealing with or provide sage advice from their own experience.

All leaders need new people in their lives. The people who got you to where you are now may not be the ones who take you where you need to go. The chief financial officer (CFO) who took you from $1 million to $5 million may not be the one who takes

> **The people who got you to where you are now may not be the ones who take you where you need to go.**

you from $5 million to $50 million. As a leader, you have to accept the fact that your CFO has his own thresholds, his own limitations, and his own issues to work through. You have to accept the fact that his perspective may be different from yours.

People You Will Encounter

There are many types of people who regularly cross the path of a leader. As you climb the ladder that you're on, you'll encounter people who are:

1. Where you used to be.

2. People who are going where you're going.

3. People who are in the place that you want to be.

Many of the difficulties that you'll encounter come from not knowing how to deal with the issues and situations raised by these different groups. When we don't know how to disengage and engage with people, it causes pain. Knowing more about these eight particular types of people can help you to deal with them appropriately:

1. Positive and negative people

2. People you have outgrown

3. People who are tied to yesterday's solutions

4. "That's not my job" people

5. People who have not moved on

6. People who can give you new perspective

7. People you can be transparent with

8. People who can celebrate your success

1. You'll encounter both **positive and negative people**. It's easy to recognize positive people; they are the ones who add value to your life. As you move up your ladder, it's important to have positive people around you. We are all built with a need for approval

> **When we don't know how to disengage and engage with people, it causes pain.**

and we want to be around people who add value by agreeing with us. It's also important to understand that agreement is not always positive and disagreement is not always negative; people can disagree with us and still add value.

But there are some people who will not agree with us at all. What can you do about these people? What strategy can you use with them? I heard one very insightful remark from the former president of Kenya. During our discussion, he made the comment, "To appease everybody is to invite trouble."

When a company or an organization grows, you will find yourself appeasing fewer people. Appeasement means that you have to find the middle of the road. The more you travel in the middle of the road, the more mediocrity you're going to produce. Excellence is found on the edges, never in the middle. Saying "yes" to one group or one person and "no" to another invites challenges on each side.

Many times, when a negative person gives you their opinion, they expect you to follow through. That's why it's important to be around people who are willing to give you input without a demanding spirit. These are the positive people, the ones who will add value and help you get where you want to go.

> **Excellence is found on the edges, never in the middle.**

2. You must also deal with **people you have outgrown**. Growing is necessary; it's what keeps you moving. There will be folks who started the journey with you that you will outdistance. Maybe there's someone who was an integral part of your organization who just hasn't grown with you. People have to understand that if you don't grow, you've got to go.

    The same thing can happen in a church. Perhaps you began with 25, 30, or even 100 people in your congregation. As you expanded to two or more services and added many more people, you might find that the elders, board members or other leaders who accompanied you are not the same ones who will take you where you need to go. As a leader, you have to accept those facts.

> **People have to understand that if you don't grow, you've got to go.**

3. **People who are tied to yesterday's solutions** are another concern. Dealing with the "old guard" is an issue that every leader has to wrestle with. In the early stages of an organization, we throw people

at issues. When you began your church, you just wanted someone to play the keyboard. You weren't concerned about the person's musical pedigree. If you and your son started a landscaping business, for instance, you're not looking for people with vast experience. You're just looking

Dealing with the "old guard" is an issue that every leader has to wrestle with.

for someone who is breathing, who can come to work and push a lawn mower. So maybe you just hire your neighbor's son, who is also your son's friend.

After a certain amount of growth, we begin refining our approach or expertise. When that happens, that's when we realize that the people we have doing the work are not working out. Maybe they don't understand what you

Yesterday's solutions have become today's problems.

want, don't want to learn contemporary worship songs, or wonder what's wrong with the way they've always done things. What do you do with those people now? Yesterday's solutions have become today's problems.

And because the young man you hired to push the lawnmower is your son's friend, your son may not like it when you let him go. Your neighbor may not like it either. Solving issues about yesterday's solutions are often complicated.

4. Then there are the **"that's not my job" people**. When you hire people, they're typically tied to job descriptions. At higher levels, you are less concerned with job descriptions than you are with the three essential factors of:

   • Character

- Competency

- Chemistry

Competency is about the skills, the training, and the experience required to get the job done. Character is about integrity. Bill Hybels describes integrity as what you do when there's nobody watching you. You want to know that you can trust this person.

Chemistry is the one characteristic that can really cause issues. It

You want people who take ownership of the situation instead of saying, "That's not my job."

asks, "Does this person fit in?" "Can they get along with other people?" Carly Fiorina was the first outsider to lead Hewlett Packard. When she left, many people attributed her departure to chemistry. She just didn't fit in with the culture of HP.

Southwest Airlines is a prime example of the great results you can achieve when employees have the right blend of competency, character and chemistry. A man called the Southwest Airlines ticket counter in Dallas concerned about his elderly mother's ability to change planes in Tulsa. The ticket agent who took the call volunteered to drive the woman to the airport and fly with her from Dallas to Tulsa after his shift was over, just to ensure that she made the connection.

You want people like that, people who aren't restricted by the circumstances under which they were hired. You want people who take ownership of the situation instead of saying, "That's not my job."

5. You also have to cope with **people who have not moved on**. A leader is always dynamic, while organizations tend to be static.

When the vision and the movement of the leader do not mirror the vision and movement of the organization, they're out of sync with each other. We call that tension a lack of organizational congruence or alignment.

Carly Fiorina's vision of merging HP and Compaq caused a great deal of organizational tension. She had to battle employees, shareholders and even the board members. Her vision was out of sync with the organization.

When you have moved on and your organization has not, you have to figure out who is going to take the journey with you and who is not. You have to think about where you're going and who can help you to get there.

6. It's also important that you find **people who can give you new perspective.** The most productive time of a new employee in any organization – secular or sacred – is the first three months. After that, they do not add the same value. In the first three months, they give you perspective by questioning the way you do things. They might say, "Didn't I just fill out a form that asked me for this same information?" They find redundancies, they look for duplication, and they look

> **...you have to figure out who is going to take the journey with you and who is not.**

for ineffectiveness. They find more effective ways to do things, they bring new ideas with them. After three months, they know survival involves falling in step, so their DNA becomes that of the organization.

When I was president of a college and hired people, I always had a conversation with a new employee and their supervisor.

I'd bring them together on the first day and encourage the new person to ask questions and tell the supervisor not to be threatened by the questions. I'd tell them that those questions will help us to reconfigure and reinvent ourselves, and help us to make improvements. New people bring a perspective that others cannot give you because they see things at another level. Whether they're internal or external, you'll be able to recognize these change agents immediately by the fresh perspective they offer your organization.

7. It's equally important to have **people you can be transparent with.** As you rise in leadership, it becomes increasingly difficult to find people you can talk to about your inner issues. There are fewer and fewer people you can be transparent with, reveal your fears to, and have them listen to your concerns. Since these are not issues you can talk about with just anybody, you need a few people in your life that you can talk to.

> **New people bring a perspective that others cannot give you because they see things at another level.**

Chances are that the people you had conversations with two years ago may not be the same people you'll be having conversations with in years to come.

Why is it so difficult to find people to talk to? It's because the stakes are higher. When your landscaping company was just two men and a truck, you could talk about anything while you're driving down the road. But when you have 10 trucks and 100 employees, you're not going to talk to everyone about the equipment you're going to buy, about your plans to leverage your business, or about who you're going to let go because they're not working out.

There are fewer people who understand the reality of your position.

You can find a lot of people when you're are at the two-men-in-a-truck level. But you're going to have fewer people available when the organization expands. It really can be lonely at the top – but it doesn't have to be.

8. You should also **find people who can celebrate your successes.** The Scriptures tell us to weep with those who weep and rejoice with those who rejoice. Unfortunately, people find it easier to weep with

> **There are fewer people who understand the reality of your position.**

those who weep than to rejoice with those who are rejoicing.

Let's say that while both of us started organizations at the same time, your organization took off but mine is struggling. It's very difficult for me to have the type of relationship with you where I can celebrate and rejoice with you.

You want people who will say, "Yeah man! It's great that you're doing well!" You want people who can be the wind beneath your wings, who can cheer you along, who won't get jealous or

> **You want people who can help you celebrate your journey.**

envious, who won't disengage from you because you're doing well. You want people who can help you celebrate your journey.

People Principles

Every leader is tempted to ignore or dismiss one particular type of person. We dream about how much easier life would be without an especially challenging soul. Or how much better things could be if we cloned someone who is full of new ideas or is always encouraging.

But the fact is, we need different types of people in our lives. Rather than avoiding people, leaders must focus on them. Jack Welch understood the importance of people and it helped him to transform stodgy General Electric into a highly

...we need different types of people in our lives.

competitive, multi-billion dollar global enterprise. Jack Welch, who has been called one of the two greatest corporate leaders of this century, said he spent 50 percent of his time on people issues. That's taking your people seriously!

Business Week reports that Welch told his senior managers that they should be proud of everyone that reports to them. If they weren't proud of their people, they weren't setting themselves up to win.[3] And Welch established the example for his leaders to follow. He sent handwritten notes to production workers. He apologized to one executive's wife for keeping him tied up with an important presentation. He commended one of his executives who turned down a promotion that would have involved having his teenage daughter transfer to another school. In many companies, turning down a promotion is what's called "a career-limiting event." But Jack Welch called this manager up and praised him for having his priorities straight.

Jack Welch knew that the way an organization grows is by growing its people. Too many leaders think that the best way to expand a company is to have a leading-edge product or a service that blows the competition away. We try to convince ourselves that the best way to grow a congregation is to have certain programs, an inspiring service, and a magnificent building. But that's not going to produce long-term growth. To grow your church or your organization, grow your leaders in number and in depth.

Achieving growth comes from following these People Principles:

- **People Principle #1**: The way to get your organization to grow is to grow your people. The way to experience growth as a leader is to grow other leaders.

- **People Principle #2**: In addition to growing others, leaders should surround themselves with people who challenge them to grow.

- **People Principle #3**: Focusing on your organization's context, not its packaging, attracts new people.

People Principle 1: *The way to get your organization to grow is to grow your people. The way to experience growth as a leader is to grow other leaders.*

Growing people is a very holistic process. It means that you pay attention to their development in the areas of character, competency and chemistry.

- By focusing on character, you ensure that when people are making decisions, they're making ethical decisions. You're ensuring that they err on the side of losing business rather than doing shady business.

> **...the way an organization grows is by growing its people.**

- Developing competency means that you send them to classes, seminars and workshops that help them to become a better widget maker, computer person, or musician.

- You focus on chemistry by helping them to strengthen people skills, leadership skills, and management skills. Typically, people don't leave organizations because of competency issues. They leave because they don't fit in with the culture, because they either don't know how or don't want to make these types of changes. Most people I've had to release fall into this category.

Growing people has to be a holistic effort. Many companies have on-site fitness facilities and wellness benefits, but imagine if your organization sponsored a marriage retreat for employees. If an employee's marriage is strong, won't he or she be more productive? If an employee isn't distracted by a divorce, won't she give the job her full attention? Isn't it better if your employee isn't working another job just to make the child support payments? Growing people means caring for the many facets of their being. After all, you want the whole person coming to work every day.

> **To grow your church or your organization, grow your leaders in number and in depth.**

People Principle #2: *In addition to growing others, leaders should surround themselves with people who challenge them to grow.*

Everyone is familiar with the undesirable type of person known as a "yes man." Only concerned with protecting their status and position, they never consider disagreeing with their leaders. Have you ever considered what your life would be like if you were surrounded by "yes men?"

> **If we only surround ourselves with people like us, our weaknesses are never challenged.**

If we only surround ourselves with people like us, our weaknesses are never challenged. Because we never complement our weaknesses within the organization, it leads to further weakness. That is why John

Maxwell says, "Staff your weaknesses." Find out where you're weak and hire people with strengths in those areas. Most pastors are not good with finances. We went to school to study theology, not management. As a result, we don't know how to read an audit and we don't know how to answer a CPA's questions. If that's you, stop pretending and hire someone with that competency.

Every time you hire, you should be looking for someone who is better than you. If you want to stay where you are and make lateral moves, hire people just like you. People who are just like you will never challenge you to grow. When Scripture talks about iron sharpening iron[4], it's talking about the need to have people who will challenge your thinking. You should gather people around

> **What attracts people is becoming part of an organization that's going somewhere, that's doing something, that's changing the world.**

you who think the ideas that you haven't, people who will challenge the status quo. Give these people permission to speak honestly so that you grow. You don't have to agree about everything. You might come away saying, "Well, we didn't agree but it sure gave me something to think about."

You have to be secure enough about your weaknesses to let someone else do it. Don't pretend that you have to do everything yourself. Insecure people will hire people who are beneath them. Secure leaders always get people who are better than they are. I can walk into any church or organization and determine how secure the primary leader is. If he has gathered eagles around him, I know he's an eagle. If he's got turkeys around him, I don't care how much he says he's an eagle. He's just a better turkey.

The Company You Keep

It is better to be alone than in the wrong company.

Tell me who your best friends are, and I will tell you who you are. If you run with wolves, you will learn how to howl. But, if you associate with eagles, you will learn how to soar to great heights. "A mirror reflects a man's face, but what he is really like is shown by the kind of friends he chooses." The simple but true fact of life is that you become like those with whom you closely associate – for the good and the bad.

The less you associate with some people, the more your life will improve. Any time you tolerate mediocrity in others, it increases your mediocrity. An important attribute in successful people is their impatience with negative thinking and negative acting people. As you grow, your associates will change. Some of your friends will not want you to go on. They will want you to stay where they are. Friends that don't help you climb will want you to crawl. Your friends will stretch your vision or choke your dream. Those that don't increase you will eventually decrease you.

Consider this:

• Never receive counsel from unproductive people.

• Never discuss your problems with someone incapable of contributing to the solution, because those who never succeed themselves are always first to tell you how. Not everyone has a right to speak into your life. You are certain to get the worst of the bargain when you exchange ideas with the wrong person.

• Don't follow anyone who's not going anywhere. With some people you spend an evening: with others you invest it.

• Be careful where you stop to inquire for directions along the road of life.

Wise is the person who fortifies his life with the right friendships.

- Anonymous

People Principle #3: *Focusing on your organization's context, not its packaging, attracts new people.*

Tom Peters says that your company will never experience a talent shortage as long as it's a great place to work. A growing organization ends up attracting people; they don't have to hire people from cold resumes. Growing organizations and churches have people who want to be a part of them.

It's not the stock options, the fringe benefits, or the salary that attract people. It's not the product or service you're providing either. What attracts people is becoming part of an **It's about value, respect and significance.** organization that's going somewhere, that's doing something, that's changing the world.

Apple's co-founder, Steve Jobs, was trying to convince John Sculley to leave his job as senior vice president of PepsiCo to become the CEO of Apple. Sculley wasn't particularly interested in leaving a secure position at Pepsi to run this brand new company. Jobs changed that by asking him, "Do you want to spend the rest of your life selling sugared water or do you want a chance to change the world?" Being part of a company that was doing something important is what attracted John Sculley to Apple.

Herb Kelleher, the founder and chairman of Southwest Airlines, says they probably have 25 applicants for every open job[5]. That's not because they've been the only airline that's been consistently profitable. It's because people want to be connected to a company that makes them feel fulfilled in their work.

Ritz Carlton is another example. Their employees are all empowered to make decisions to ensure that guests are satisfied. When you talk

> **When we grow others, we are also growing ourselves.**

to them about a problem, they don't pass the buck to the manager. Instead, they immediately take ownership and follow up. That attitude is apparent in their credo, "Ladies and gentlemen serving ladies and gentlemen."

It's about value, respect and significance. Why is it that some companies in Silicon Valley have no trouble attracting people in spite of that area's talent shortage? It's because people want to be connected to an organization that values them, that gives them important work to do, and that treats them with respect.

Taking Appropriate Action

As a leader, you need many different kinds of people. Often, problems arise when you're not certain how to engage and disengage with the

> **A leader does three things: they know, they grow and they show.**

people around you. I've found it helpful to interact with people by determining whether this is someone who I can assist with their leadership growth, someone who can grow alongside me, or someone who will help me to develop my leadership potential.

We engage each of these people differently.

- Reach *down* to those we can assist. A leader is someone who shares what they've learned with others. They use their own growth to help others to grow; they purposefully mentor others. When we grow others, we are also growing ourselves.

A leader does three things: they know, they grow and they show. Knowing means getting information. By using the information you acquire, you grow and develop yourself. That alone doesn't make you a leader. You have to show someone else what you know to be a leader.

Giving away what you've learned sounds odd. Why would you share your hard-earned secrets with someone else? Because you never lose by giving away power; the best use of power is empowering others. When you empower someone else, you've made a friend for life.

> **...you never lose by giving away power; the best use of power is empowering others.**

- **Reach *out* to those who are where you are presently.** If both of our companies have 100 trucks, we can commiserate about our troubles and rejoice in our successes. During this conversation between peers, you are both learning from the other person's experience. You may not be adding a lot of value to them and they may not be adding a lot of value to you. You're just experiencing cohesiveness, camaraderie, and collegiality by being transparent with each other.

- **Reach *up* to those who are where you want to be.** It's important that we also get assistance from those who are where we want to be. Put yourself in environments that let these people recognize who you are, and let them know that you'd like to benefit from their knowledge and experience.

> **Disengaging from people is difficult, it's painful, and it's messy.**

It's this last category that can be somewhat painful. That's because you have to disengage with people who have brought you where you are in order to engage with the people who can take you up.

Leaders only grow to the threshold of their pain.

If you've been spending time with a new group, you don't have the time to devote to the people you used to see. If you were with people who ran small companies and now your company is growing, you're busy engaging with people running other growing companies.

Disengaging from people is difficult, it's painful, and it's messy. It's painful because you really care about these people and may not want to disengage. It's painful because you realize that unless you disengage, you'll never be able to have the time to engage new people. And it's also painful because you realize that you may never see these different groups together because their worlds and realities are so different. It's painful because the people that you're disengaging from will not be able to understand why you've disengaged from them. It's painful all the way around. But remember, unless you are willing to endure these pains, your own growth as a leader will be limited. Leaders only grow to the threshold of their pain.

Teaching Points

- All leaders need new people in their lives. The people who got you where you are now may not be the ones who take you where you need to go.

- Many of the difficulties that you'll encounter come from not knowing how to deal with issues and situations raised by different types of people.

  - You'll encounter people who agree and disagree with you. Agreement is not always positive and disagreement is not always negative. People can disagree with you and still add value.

  - You'll have to deal with people you've outgrown, those who you've outpaced.

  - People who are still tied to yesterday's solutions can become today's problems.

  - There are also people who will only stay within the boundaries of their job description and not take ownership of situations.

  - A leader must deal with static people and static organizations. When they're not moving in sync, the tension is a lack of organizational congruence.

  - People new to your organization can offer you new perspective on redundancies and ineffectiveness during their first 90 days.

  - As you rise in leadership, there are few people who understand the reality of your position. So it's important to find people you can be transparent with about your inner issues.

- You should also have people who can celebrate your successes without being jealous or envious.

- We need different types of people in our lives. As we focus on growing people, the organization will experience growth. Focus on growing people in the areas of character, chemistry and competency.

- Surround yourself with people who will challenge your own growth. If you only hire people like you, it never complements your weaknesses within the organization.

- As long as your organization values people by giving them important work to do and treating them with respect, you'll never experience a talent shortage.

- When interacting with people, we should:

  - Reach down to share our growth with other leaders, those who are potential leaders and those who are where we used to be.

  - Reach out to peers who are where we are presently.

  - Reach up to those who are where we'd like to be.

- Unless you're willing to engage with new people and disengage with others, your own leadership growth will be limited.

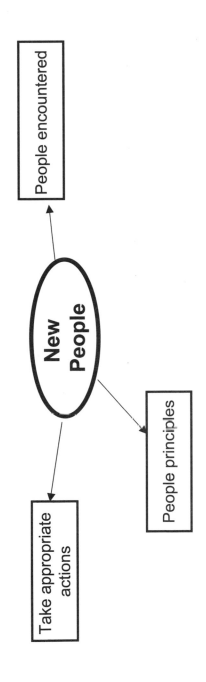

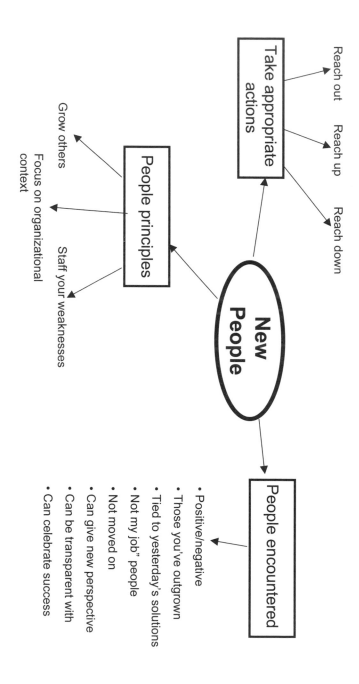

Take appropriate actions
- Reach out
- Reach up
- Reach down

People principles
- Grow others
- Focus on organizational context
- Staff your weaknesses

New People

People encountered
- Positive/negative
- Those you've outgrown
- Tied to yesterday's solutions
- Not my job" people
- Not moved on
- Can give new perspective
- Can be transparent with
- Can celebrate success

2

New Pains

God whispers to us in our pleasures, speaks in our conscience,

but shouts in our pains; it is his megaphone to rouse a deaf world.

– C. S. Lewis, Author, "The Problem of Pain"

As the front door closed behind her, Jill dropped her briefcase, switched on the living room light, and sank wearily into her favorite armchair. Leaving for work in the dark and coming home after sunset was becoming a routine. With local fire codes forcing the center to turn away increasing numbers of needy families, she continued waging an uphill battle to expand the facility to meet the needs of the community.

At the end of yet another long day, she wondered if the expansion strategy was taking the center "one step forward and two steps back." After weeks of frustrating paperwork and endless board meetings, the grant proposals to deliver the needed funds were finally in the hands of the government decision makers. But she now awaited news of the proposals without the much-needed support of her assistant director, Ann.

Together, Ann and Jill had raised the funds to start the center and enthusiastically championed its activities. Almost as the new expansion plans started, Ann began calling out sick frequently and becoming increasingly critical of the expansion. Jill finally asked for Ann's resignation after weeks of painful conversations and her own internal debates. Taking a pile of resumes from her briefcase, she wondered why she hadn't seen earlier signs of this problem and hoped she could locate a replacement to help her manage the expansion.

Today's leaders are feeling pains they've never felt before. The exploding rate of change is causing some of these pains. Rapid technological innovation brings new pains, finding honest and competent people bring new pains, and being a global entity operating in different cultures brings new pains. For pastors, there are the pains of misplaced leaders, building programs, increases and decreases in membership, and more or less money.

The increased pace of change gives everything a shorter shelf life. Not long ago, when someone got a job, they were content to work there

Today's leaders are feeling pains they've never felt before.

until they retired with a gold Rolex. Now, it's estimated that a Generation Xer will make seven to 10 job changes in a lifetime. And people are relocating as often as they're changing jobs, with the average American projected to live in seven houses.

Change isn't the only cause of our pains. The higher your position, the more pains you have to bear. If you went through graduate school, for example, you endured pains that someone with a high school diploma never encountered. If you're the local mayor, your pains come from being accountable, critiqued and criticized by the people of your town.

When you become governor, you have more pains. If you happen to rise from governor to president, you have some *major* pains!

Many people don't seek public office because they're unwilling to put up with the pains of those positions. We all have thresholds of pain – both consciously and unconsciously – that cause us to say, "That's not worth it." When you're the CEO, you're never off. You may be out of the office but you're always on call. You have pains that most people never understand.

Think about the number of people who wish they could be Bill Gates. There's no shortage of people dreaming of being one of the wealthiest men in the world or imagining their picture on the cover of *Time* as Man of the Year. They don't think about

> **When you're the CEO, you're never off.**

the price Bill Gates pays or the pains he endures. They don't imagine themselves in his shoes during the Microsoft antitrust trial. They don't aspire to be the Microsoft CEO who had his proposal turned down by AOL and then watched them announce a partnership with their rival, Google. They don't consider that Bill Gates became Man of the Year for his philanthropic work, not for creating a well-known software company. They've never imagined his pains.

Necessary Pains

Some pains are quite normal. Scripture tells us not be surprised or dismayed by the "fiery ordeals" we encounter. As leaders, we should also accept certain pains as part of the job; they just come with the territory.

Obviously, we're not referring here to the pains of wrongdoing or the pains of injury or illness. We're talking about the pains that come as you begin fulfilling your vision. In these cases, the pains you experience can be regarded as similar to those of childbirth. They may not be pleasant, you may experience discomfort and distress, but because you have a goal and a vision that you're focused on, these pains can seem relatively small in the grander scheme.

Often, pains come because of the great care and diligence, the painstaking efforts we're investing in our work. When we take pains with our work, we can expect to get some pains in return. To grow as a leader, you must be willing to embrace these pains. It's a job requirement. In fact, your willingness to handle the pains you encounter will determine the level of leadership to which you'll rise.

I know some great preachers who will always pastor small churches because they cannot handle the issues and challenges that come with larger ones. There are other pastors who end up in larger churches because they have a greater capacity for handling pain. They may not be as talented as the small-church pastor; they just have a higher pain threshold.

> **...your willingness to handle the pains you encounter will determine the level of leadership to which you'll rise.**

It's very important for leaders to understand why these painful circumstances we encounter exist in the first place. Let's face it; if we didn't want the pains, we'd take a 9-to-5 job or settle for a lesser position. While pain may not be what motivates us, it's our willingness to handle pains that determines our level of leadership.

For example, if you leave a 9-to-5 job to start a fast-food franchise, that brings all kinds of new pains with it. It challenges your family life in new ways because you have to work longer hours. If the business continues to grow, you might think about starting another franchise, which is another level of pain. Some people wouldn't consider that second franchise; others wouldn't even want the first one. To them, it isn't worth it. It's just too painful.

Varieties of Pains

The force of a bullet strikes you like a sledgehammer, knocking you backward. Your windows vibrate to the rumble of distant thunder and approaching storm clouds. Pains come at many levels. What types of pains do leaders typically experience?

At various times, you'll encounter:

- *External pains.* These pains are the approaching storm clouds. They tend to have distant causes, like cultural changes, external pressures, and competitive realities.

- *Organizational pains.* As you respond to external realities, you'll find yourself dealing with organizational conflict and making decisions that involve increasingly higher stakes.

- *Internal pains.* These are the bullets that come as you deal with various issues – painful realizations about yourself, your personal boundaries and your own inadequacies.

External Pains

Leading in a changing culture. The changing cultural norms of today and tomorrow raise questions about how things get done. It doesn't matter how slowly or how quickly a familiar cultural landscape is transformed into an unfamiliar seascape, it still creates pains.

For example, the hierarchical culture of the boss telling people what to do has fallen by the wayside, replaced by the consensus building of a collaborative culture. No longer is it enough for a CEO on the 18th floor to send a directive. Now he must get buy-in from the vice presidents, they get buy-in from their managers, who get it from the supervisors and foremen, who get the buy-in of the people on the floor. Tom Friedman talks about this in *The World is Flat*; the hierarchies, the pyramids, and the flow charts that described how things got done don't work any more.

> **Cultural shifts demand new ways of looking at things and new vocabularies.**

Cultural shifts demand new ways of looking at things and new vocabularies. Virtual teams, collaborative groups, and task forces are emphasized with this new language. Products are marketed in entirely new ways. While you're traveling on Delta, they're marketing Starbucks. While you're at Starbucks, they're marketing the *Atlanta Journal-Constitution*. Everything is more tightly interwoven. When you rent a movie, they're advertising TV programs, and TV programs are trying to get visits to Web sites.

There's a new team with new delivery systems integrating the vertical smokestacks of yesterday. In times past, when the majority of business was transacted locally, if you weren't in Atlanta, we wouldn't work together. Now, cell phones, e-mail and digital networks have tied together people from across the globe. For example, I live in Atlanta, GA, my writer is in northern New Jersey, and this book is published in Chicago, IL.

While they provide new capabilities, new delivery systems cause pains as well. There are large pains and there are smaller pains. For example, when you're having conference calls with your multinational associates, what time zone gets preference? And when you're transacting commerce, what exchange rate do you use? That's part of transitioning to new cultural norms.

No control over external realities. The pace of progress demands faster and more proactive action. This frantic pace brings with it the realization that – despite your intensive market analysis, demographic studies and strategic plans – you're no longer in the driver's seat with both hands firmly on the wheel.

Sometimes, the realization occurs in small, yet sudden ways. A local expansion widens a roadway, displacing smaller and older businesses as new ones open. A dependable supplier was one of those

> **The pace of progress demands faster and more proactive action.**

statistics, forcing you to find a replacement. It's happening more and more frequently, especially if that road construction happens to be making room for a new superstore.

It's painful to realize your lack of influence over issues and situations you want to retain control of, and to watch as the things you *had* control of begin wriggling from your grasp.

Competitive realities. Competitive landscapes can quickly become raging seascapes, capable of swallowing even the most legendary organizations.

Remember when AT&T was the only game in town? First, threats came from Sprint, MCI and other long-distance companies. Then, more intense competition grew from the Baby Bells that were once part of their own family. Finally, the competitive environment was completely altered, with cell phone companies, cable TV and Internet companies providing inexpensive calling plans. And now the cycle is beginning again.

Certainly, the pains of remaining relevant or competitive are no picnic; but heeding those pains can keep you from becoming irrelevant, an acquisition target, or a statistic.

Organizational Pains

Decisions with higher stakes. When I became president at Beulah Heights Bible College, our entire annual budget was under $100,000. Eventually, we progressed to budgets that were in the millions, and then multiple millions of dollars.

Every decision I made involved increasingly higher stakes. I was constantly aware that making a bad decision could result in a significant

The angst of the struggle to make the right decision always brings pains.

revenue loss or affect the jobs of the 93 people working there. The gravity of making high priority, life-and-death decisions is what ages U.S. presidents, causing them to enter the White House looking young and coming out with gray hair and bags under their eyes. It's because every stroke has to count.

Now, my pains are different. A bad business decision would only affect my family, my assistant and me. It's much different than it was at the college, when my decisions affected the lives of many more people. The angst of the struggle to make the right decision always brings pains.

Internal organizational conflict. A small organization experiences relatively little strife. The smaller numbers make it easier to manage expectations and minimize the amount of conflict that arises when people's expectations differ from what they experience.

As your organization becomes more successful and your staff expands, it's tougher to manage the conflict between expectations and reality. You also have to contend with competition among the staff, differing perspectives, a range of preferences and many more biases. The success of a growing organization brings new pains.

> **The success of a growing organization brings new pains.**

Internal Pains

Realizing our inadequacies. It happens. Despite our best research and preparation, things don't turn out like we expected. It's easy to begin to question our own competency, our mission and our judgment, especially when we hear the loud voices of our critics.

We lay awake, with the questions from our own internal critic echoing in the dark. "I should have known that. Why didn't I know that? Why did I make that choice?" Our own inadequacies bring pains.

Rising to the level of our incompetence. Every leader has their own personal glass ceiling, that place they just can't move beyond. Eventually, all of us reach the level of our incompetence described by the Peter Principle.

Maybe you've realized that you can't grow your church beyond 200 people. You average between 180 and 220, bumping up and down, up and down. It doesn't matter what you try, that's where you remain.

Perhaps your organization is stalled. Despite your research into new markets and new product launches, you can't take it any further. A growth strategy seems to elude you. It's a painful place to be.

Emerging from a painful level is possible, however, if we're willing to challenge our own thinking, as described in the chapter on "New Perspectives" in this book.

Disengaging from familiar people. A number of times, I've had to part ways or let go of people who accompanied me on my journey. I've hired a lot of people and I've fired a lot of people, too. It raises questions about loyalty, about entitlement, and about friendship. It's always painful; you always hurt for people.

Emerging from a painful level is possible

Separations are often unavoidable business realities. When Delta Airlines filed for bankruptcy, they had to go through the pain of letting thousands of people go. They couldn't keep doing business as usual. As part of their restructuring, Ford also cut thousands of jobs. Despite the reality of the numbers, it's never an easy decision.

Pastors know the pain of separation quite well. It's particularly painful when it involves good, faithful people. "She was our first Sunday school teacher. He's been my deacon and my organist since we were 25. They always gave sacrificially and hung in there with us. But now we need someone who can take us to another level."

Separations are often unavoidable business realities.

Letting go of people creates all kinds of pains, but making those changes is frequently a requirement of moving forward. That pain is part of the challenge of leadership.

Needing new people. A growing organization needs new talent and new people. That's always a challenge that brings new pains.

There are the pains of deciding what type of skills and characteristics are required, what certifications and education are needed. You have to conduct the interviews to determine if this person has the right mix of character, chemistry and competency

> **Letting go of people creates all kinds of pains**

to fit in with your organization. If you've just separated from the person that was in the position you're filling, that adds additional pain.

An inability to articulate internal realities. Developing a vision can be a very intuitive, creative process. While the vision is percolating inside our heart and our spirit, we know something exciting is happening. Early in that process, it's hard to get our minds and words synchronized with what we're seeing.

I've seen this a lot with leaders, especially with pastors. They have an inspiring, exciting idea about where they want to go. Many times, they find it difficult to articulate. When they do attempt to express it, it's

> **...it's hard to get our minds and words synchronized with what we're seeing.**

sometimes vague, general and amorphous – even to them! That's a frustrating and painful place to be.

Transformational Pains

When Lou Gerstner became the chairman and CEO of IBM in 1993, the company was in trouble. During his first meeting, the leadership team discussed IBM's strategy. When that eight-hour meeting was over, Gerstner says he didn't understand a thing; it was almost as though the other leaders spoke a different language.

That meeting, as painful as it was, revealed to him exactly what he was up against in making the company profitable. Eventually, he had

All leaders must bear the pains of criticism.

to transform IBM's powerful culture, a culture that made it both famous and successful in the 1960s and '70s.

Imagine being a company outsider and having to transform an icon like IBM. How did he do it? Gerstner made friends with his pains. He had to embrace the pain of transforming the famous IBM culture, the pain of centralizing what had become a very individualistic operation, and the pain of flying in the face of many other things that were considered standard-operating procedure before he arrived. By embracing these pains, he turned IBM around.

Athletes are always playing while they are hurting. They know they have to make friends with their pains. One pro-football player says that playing is like "being in a car wreck every day[6]." Why do they continue doing it? Because they love playing; they understand that their pains are the price they pay.

Embracing your pains is never easy. All leaders must bear the pains of

New pains will always be a part of your life as you continue climbing the ladder to your destiny.

criticism. You cannot be a leader and avoid being criticized. Everything the president of the United States says and does is intensely scrutinized. Every Sunday talk show dissects his

policies and actions. It takes thick skin to be the president.

When Princess Camilla visited America, the press criticized her for what she wore and what she didn't wear. They wrote about how many changes of clothes she brought for an eight-day visit. Imagine, being Camilla and reading an article that said she looks "frumpy." That's painful. But if you want to be a princess or a president, that's what you have to deal with.

Making friends with your pains is part of leadership. Our pains tell us we are moving in the right direction. New pains will always be a part of your life as you continue climbing the ladder to your destiny.

Teaching Points

- The exploding rate of change is causing new pains, giving everything a shorter shelf life.

- The higher your position, the more pains you must bear.

- Your willingness to handle the pains you'll encounter determines the level of leadership to which you'll rise.

- You'll encounter external pains, organizational pains, and internal pains.

- External pains come from changing cultural norms, a lack of control over external realities, and competitive pressures.

  - Changing cultural norms raise questions about how things should be done.

  - A lack of control includes your lack of influence over issues and situations you want to control, as well as a loss of control over things you once controlled.

  - Competitive landscapes can quickly be transformed into raging seascapes.

- Organizational pains include decisions with higher stakes and organizational conflicts.

  - Rising in leadership involves making decisions with larger budgets and the ability to affect the lives of many more people.

  - As an organization grows, it becomes more difficult to manage expectations and minimize organizational conflict.

- Internal pains include personal inadequacies, rising to the level of our incompetence, disengaging from familiar people, needing new people and an inability to articulate internal realities.

- Despite our best efforts, things may not turn out as we expected, causing us to question our choices.

- We may reach a level that we simply cannot move beyond.

- Separation from people we know is often an unavoidable reality.

- We also experience the pains of needing and finding the right people.

- Our inability to express our own vision can also be painful.

- Embracing your pains is a necessary part of leadership.

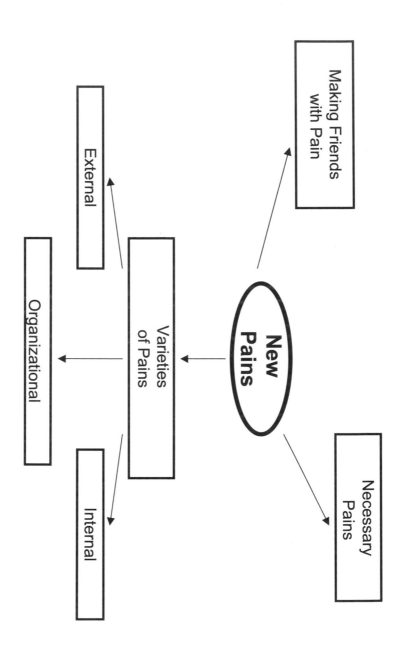

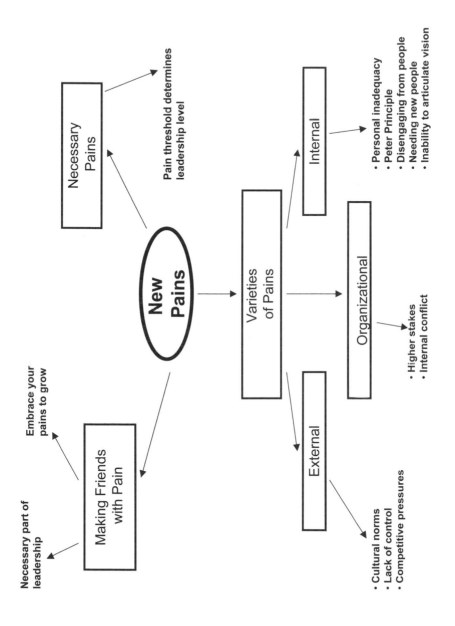

3

New Places

"The next sea change is upon us. We must recognize this change as an opportunity to take our offerings to the next level..."

– Bill Gates, co-founder and chairman, Microsoft

Blogging. Until a few weeks ago, Jill had never heard the term. Since the board's recent decision to use this new Internet technology to publicize her non-profit group's activities on the Web, she's read and talked about little else. Apparently, having a blog – which is short for "Web log" – is the latest in high-tech business tools. Written in an informal style, almost like an online diary, they can give any organization – including big bloggers like GM and Google – a more human voice.

Jill hoped her forays into the strange land of technology were over when she launched the group's Web site. Now, she's puzzling over how a blog will connect people with the charitable work they're doing in the community and wondering where she'll find the talent needed to keep the content fresh and interesting. Smiling to herself, she thinks that one of the kids skateboarding a few floors down could probably wrap up this blog thing much more quickly and capably.

Church and business leaders around the world are finding themselves in places that are brand new to them. Many churches and organizations are journeying to new places because of the needs arising in their communities. They may or may not be creating Web blogs, but they are reaching out in ways that a few years ago were not even on their radar.

Business leaders are also moving to new places. They're finding themselves in new places in their own leadership journeys, new places with their products, new places with their mode of delivery, and new places in customer service.

Going to new places is good. The American Indians understood this. If they didn't like someone, they'd curse them by saying, "May you stay in the same place." When they said this, they were obviously thinking about more than your geography. They

Remaining in the same place produces mediocrity.

were wishing you a stagnant personal journey, a family that wouldn't grow, a future that was a lot less than prosperous. They were wishing that you would remain in the same condition, without moving, without growing, and without changing.

Remaining in the same place produces mediocrity. Many years ago, farmers discovered that when land is forced to produce the same crops year after year, it affects the soil by robbing it of essential nutrients. To continue producing good crops in the days before fertilizer, they just changed what they planted in an area or let a piece of farmland rest for a season, giving the soil a chance to renew itself. Change was regarded as a good and necessary thing.

Getting to New Places

It's a leader's nature to seek out and journey to new places. In order to reach these new places, a few things are required. We must:

- Develop a clear vision of our destination

- Disengage with activities and people not headed in that direction

- Connect with others who are already at your desired destination

Having a clear vision is a necessity. Once your destination is clear, you're more inclined to find the resources that can take you where you want to go. For instance, if your vision is growing a business that develops Web sites that offer safe

Having a clear vision is a necessity.

on-line shopping, that goal drives your thinking and your activities. You won't allow yourself to be sidetracked by seminars for video-game developers or industry associations for shoe salesmen.

I'm finding that more and more leaders are getting clearer about their destinations. They're defining where they want to go and investing the resources that will take them there. Unfortunately, a clear vision is not the only requirement for reaching your destination. Some leaders know that they want to go west, for example, but they're still lingering at the eastern seaboard. Occasionally, they gaze at the westbound train that's headed toward the frontier that they're dreaming about.

No amount of wishing, dreaming and visioning is ever going to get them where they want to go. Reaching our destination requires that we disengage from the place we're at and the people we're with before we can catch the train headed in the right direction.

How important is disengaging? For Intel, disengaging is probably what maintained the company's profitability – and possibly their existence – in the extremely competitive chip market.

In the early 1980s, most of Intel's top executives didn't see the need to change a thing. At the time, Intel was probably the leading provider of memory chips and was making about $1 billion a year. Andy Grove, who was president of Intel, and CEO

Don't think that disengaging is easy.

Gordon Moore, knew the industry was about to undergo drastic changes. Japanese firms were starting to make the same chips available so cheaply that they would soon become commodities. By 1984, Intel's profits fell below $2 million[7].

Don't think that disengaging is easy. In his book, *Only the Paranoid Survive*, Grove says that he knew that Intel had to exit that market but had trouble even getting the words out of his mouth. Over time, he was able to take the necessary, painful action of disengaging from a market that Intel had virtually created so they could move forward. Disengaging was painful all around for Intel. It meant layoffs for thousands of employees and the company's first loss since their start-up days.

Was it worth it? Let's answer one question with another one: Does the slogan, "Intel Inside" mean anything to you? Disengaging from the memory chip market is what enabled Intel to focus on the microprocessor and led to them being selected as the chip that powered IBM's new personal computer. The rest – as they say – is history. But the first step in getting there was disengaging.

You cannot remain static if you want to be moving. You have to become part of something that is moving and associate with people who are moving. If your church, company or organization is going somewhere, you'll find that people will want to be connected with you so that they can go somewhere too.

In addition to connecting yourself to people and organizations that are moving, it's important to identify, connect and seek help from people who are already at your destination.

> **You cannot remain static if you want to be moving.**

Talking with people who are where you want to go helps you to develop a much clearer vision of your destination.

Coping with the Journey

By its very nature, a journey to a new place can be uncomfortable. It's uncomfortable because you're leaving the familiar, leaving your comfort zone and traveling into the unknown.

While there may be no maps of the new places you're in, there are four principles that can help you navigate the terrain of any unfamiliar territory:

- Be ready to give up the familiar to make friends with the unfamiliar
- Develop a level of comfort with ambiguity
- Be flexible in your direction
- Emphasize seascapes over landscapes

Anytime that you journey into the unfamiliar, you experience a certain amount of angst, of concern, of nervousness. Anytime – and this is true

> **Talking with people who are where you want to go helps you to develop a much clearer vision of your destination.**

for people of faith especially – that God asks you to go to new places, you have to *give up what's become familiar and make friends with the unfamiliar.* Everything in our psyche wants to stay in the familiar; everything in God's psyche moves us to the unfamiliar.

Scripture is full of examples of this:

- Abraham, you're familiar with this land but I'm taking you into a land that you haven't seen.

- David, you're familiar with the sheep. I'm going to take you into the unfamiliar territory of kingship and politics.

- Daniel, you are familiar with working in high levels of government, but I'm going to take you into the unfamiliar place of taking a stand for righteousness.

- Peter, you're a good fisherman but I'm going to make you a fisher of men.

While everything in us wants to run toward the known and the familiar, God is always trying to take us toward the uncertain and unfamiliar. That's because it's in the uncertain, in the unfamiliar, and in the new places that we trust God in new ways.

In addition to becoming personally comfortable with your own journey to new places, you have to create an organizational culture that's ready to make friends with the unfamiliar, a culture that fosters innovative thinking, that's open to exploring new ideas and traveling to new places. Too many organizations only reward their people for staying with what's familiar.

Two years before Netscape Communications launched the first Web browser, a researcher showed a prototype to Hewlett Packard's CEO. Now, the CEO was excited about the browser concept and passed it along to the leaders of HP's computer division. When the computer division reviewed the browser, they rejected it. Why? Partly because they couldn't imagine how this new thing could help them sell computers and partly because management always stressed the importance of meeting quarterly goals over investing.

> **Everything in our psyche wants to stay in the familiar; everything in God's psyche moves us to the unfamiliar.**

Failing to make friends with the unfamiliar can be costly. While your organization needs processes, you have to be careful that you're not stifling the innovative thinking that could take you to unfamiliar places.

Google is a great example of a company that nurtures innovation. All of their engineers have one day a week to work on their own pet projects, even if what they're doing isn't directly connected to the company's efforts. If their project work prevents them from using this independent time, they can save it up and use it later. Their top executives also have office hours where employees can schedule time to discuss new ideas. And any employee can post and debate concepts for the business to consider on their online bulletin boards.

Google knows that in order for their organization to grow, they must get comfortable with the unfamiliar. You have to be willing to move into uncertainty and willing to venture into unknown territory. For example, maybe your organization has always done well with one person handling your bookkeeping. As you grow, it becomes too much work for just one or two people, so your lead bookkeeper proposes an outsourcing arrangement. You might not be comfortable with a new arrangement. You know how your people do things and are comfortable walking down the hall to their offices and asking questions. You don't know these new accountants. But if you want to continue growing, you have to be willing to walk through the unfamiliar and into growth.

Every leader also has to *cultivate a level of comfort with ambiguity*, both real and perceived. We like to think that we know where we're

> **...it's in the uncertain, in the unfamiliar, and in the new places that we trust God in new ways.**

going, but all we really have is a general direction. We are always living with the ambiguous. We may have many questions that we'd like to answer, but we just have to see what happens as the journey unfolds. You have to be comfortable about saying that you'll only be able to address some issues as you move forward. Once you reach a new milestone, you'll have other things to figure out. Your destination is always perceived; it hasn't yet become real. You may have mapped out your strategy and developed some tactics, but as your journey unfolds, situations will change in ways you cannot perceive.

Because things change during your journey, you also have to *be flexible in your direction*. Having the flexibility to make mid-course corrections and shift lanes is an important part of reaching your destination.

My own destination has been distilling itself over time. I came to America as a student and became the breakfast cook, dishwasher and janitor for my college. After I graduated, I became the assistant pastor of a church, got married, started a family, and then became the senior pastor. Then

I came to Beulah Heights Bible College as president and later became its chancellor. Now I'm writing books, speaking and consulting. I've had to become comfortable with shifting lanes and being able to make transitions. If I was not comfortable with shifting lanes, I would have gotten "arthritis of life" and gotten stuck somewhere along the way.

Have you noticed people on the highway who get stuck in the passing lane? They just stay there, cruising along. I don't ever want to get stuck in that lane because getting to new places sometimes means getting off at an exit, taking a detour and getting back on the expressway further down the road. Finding new places requires a certain amount of flexibility.

Don't underestimate the importance of making friends with the unfamiliar, being comfortable with ambiguity, and staying flexible. These are critical principles to master because you're not a pioneer traveling across the *landscape* in a covered wagon – you're the captain of a sailboat navigating the changing

> **...you have to be willing to walk through the unfamiliar and into growth.**

and uncharted waters of a *seascape*. Watching the ocean from a beach reminds us that the landscape we're standing on is stationary and static. However, just a few feet ahead, the seascape changes every second.

Leaders emphasize seascapes over landscapes. Why? Because they know that their journey is not taking them through an environment that's stationary, but one that is dynamic and ever changing. Not being prepared for a dynamic environment causes problems for many organizations.

Look at AT&T. For years, they monopolized the telecommunications industry. Even after parts of their business were broken up into regional telephone companies, they continued to operate like the monopoly they were for so many years. They just were not able to shift lanes because they still thought like a huge behemoth. In many ways, they behaved like they were living on a landscape while their industry became a seascape.

Leaders emphasize seascapes over landscapes.

Delta Airlines is another example. They're in financial trouble while cut-rate providers – like Air Tran, Southwest, Frontier, and others – are making money. The reason these companies are making money is because they're small and nimble. They continue scanning the environment and adapting to the evolving conditions around them. When the landscape changes into a seascape, they're willing to adapt and change quickly. They are like little sports cars, weaving in and out of traffic, not large tractor-trailers.

In *The World is Flat*, Tom Friedman talks about the effect of globalization. He makes the point that while many things in the global economy have changed quite rapidly, our delivery systems and methodologies have not. We have to be willing to make changes as we navigate the seascape because it's changing every second. We have to always be open to new places, to always be willing to catch the next wave.

No organization is immune to making changes. Don't think that because your church is healthy that it doesn't need to change. Reflecting on his ten-year anniversary of succeeding Chuck Swindoll as pastor of the First Evangelical Free Church, H. Dale Burke observed that healthy churches have a harder time seeing the need to change. No one may be very concerned about subtle symptoms at a healthy church. But that doesn't mean that changes aren't needed to reach a changing world[8].

Knowing that we're navigating a seascape provides some important information:

- The environment is always changing

- It's changing faster than we realize

- We're all going to new places

- We'd better be thinking about those new places so that we can make the course corrections needed to reach our destination

You'd better believe that Bill Gates is closely watching the sea changes affecting his industry and is taking action to reach his destination. To lead Microsoft in the next phase of changes being brought about by the Internet, he hired a new chief technical officer. They've already been anticipating changes in how software will be distributed, used and paid for, changes that might resemble the model that Napster made popular[9].

> **We have to be willing to make changes as we navigate the seascape because it's changing every second.**

Bill Gates has been watching sea changes for quite some time. In a recent memo to his senior executives, he mentions a memo titled, "The Internet Tidal Wave" that he wrote in 1995 forecasting how the Internet would alter the computing industry and describing what it meant for Microsoft. Bill Gates pays attention to seascapes; he knows that if he rides them, they'll take him and his company to new places.

Teaching Points

- Going to new places is a good and necessary thing. Remaining in the same place only produces mediocrity.

- Reaching new places requires developing a clear vision of your destination, disengaging with people and activities not headed in that direction, and connecting with others headed to your destination.

  - Once your destination is clear, you're more inclined to find the necessary resources.

  - Reaching the destination involves disengaging from where we are presently. We cannot remain static.

  - We must also connect with people who are already at the place we want to go.

- Going to new places is easier when we are ready to make friends with the unfamiliar, develop a level of comfort with ambiguity, are flexible, and emphasize seascapes over landscapes.

- Human nature wants to stay with what's familiar. We have to be ready to leave our comfort zone and journey into the unknown.

- We have to create organizational cultures that foster innovative thinking. Failing to do this can be costly.

- We are always living with the ambiguous, even though we like to think we know where we're headed.

- Because things may change, we have to remain flexible enough to make course corrections.

- As we make friends with the unfamiliar, we know that the stationary landscapes we knew will become the dynamic seascapes that we must navigate.

- We must be ready to catch the next wave because things are changing faster than we realize.

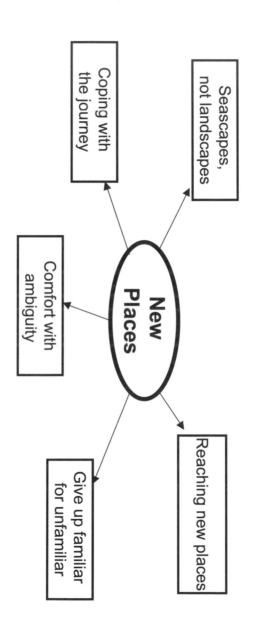

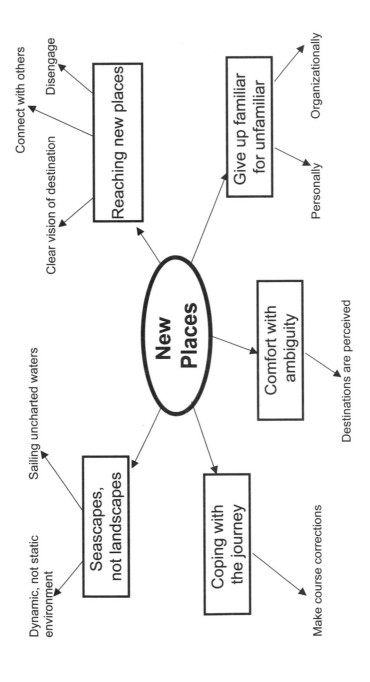

4

New Perspectives

"He not busy being born is busy dying."

– Bob Dylan, Singer/Songwriter, "It's Alright Ma (I'm Only Bleeding)"

The glowing digital clock signaled 3 a.m. Unable to sleep, Youth Pastor Joe quietly tiptoed downstairs, unplugged his guitar from its amp, and strummed quietly. Across town, Jake Barrett, the church's senior pastor, revisited the same board meeting as his youth pastor.

Joe's quiet energy and passion had invigorated the church's teen and college-aged youth. Still, the board was divided over his proposal for a Friday night youth service, voicing concern that an evening gathering would deplete Sunday morning attendance. Joe described similar gatherings that had increased overall interest in spiritual matters.

Staring at his guitar, he wondered why no amount of information seemed to sway the board, why they refused to even experiment. In his kitchen, Jake questioned his own reservations, asking himself why he resisted this new idea despite the inability to sustain the interest of the church youth before Joe's arrival. As the clock glowed past 4 a.m., both men sat pondering in silence.

E very leader needs to be able to see things differently, to think outside the box. The business world values fresh perspectives because it's being different, being ahead of the pack that creates demand for products and services. When the leaders of churches and non-profit organizations develop and introduce fresh insights, it brings growth.

How important is a new perspective? In *The Effective Executive*, Peter Drucker tells of a medical supply company knocked from the top position in its industry. The company leaders were shocked because their products were technically superior to those of the rival who beat them.

Eventually, they learned that their successful competitor didn't win by spending a huge research budget on technical breakthroughs. Instead of battling them on their own turf, they sent their people into the hospitals and doctor's offices that used these products, encouraging

> **...getting perspective means forcing ourselves to think in new ways.**

them to observe and listen, not to sell. The information and fresh insights they gained by learning about their customers' environment and challenges led to new perspectives that made them the industry's provider of choice.

The Genesis of Perspective

Gaining new perspectives is always rewarding. But getting perspective means forcing ourselves to think in new ways. Our tried-and-true methods of thinking won't lead to finding different methods of competing or fresh paths for serving. Since it's important to be aware of how we developed our current thinking, let's examine the six primary

origins of our perspective:
1. Family
2. Friends
3. Foes
4. Culture
5. Education
6. Ancient wisdom

1. Our **family** is the first core group that teaches us how to think something through. This is where we get our core values, our history, our prejudices, fears, biases and preferences.

2. The second group that becomes important to us is our **friends**. When we interact with our friends, they bring all the influences of their families with them. If you have three good friends, all of them bring their own universes to the table. When you're talking, they'll say, "My mom does this," "My dad says this," "We would never do that," or "Why don't you do that?" Even as kids, they help us think through things because they bring us another perspective.

3. Then there are our **foes**, our enemies. These are people who don't like you, don't care for you, who don't wish you the very best. When they raise issues that you know don't have your best intent in mind, it helps you to see things in a different perspective. Perhaps you are in a meeting

You begin to keep your friends close and your enemies closer

and you know that there's somebody there to undercut you. They are not there for you; they are there to challenge you by raising issues about your department. This is just the way they think. The way to win with this enemy is to think like the enemy. So, you begin to keep your friends close and your enemies closer – and that gives you a new perspective.

4. The **culture** that we're in also gives us perspective. By culture, I'm talking about regions of the country and parts of the world. If you're from the northeast and I'm from the south, our cultures are different. We will interact differently, think differently, and emphasize things differently.

5. Our **education** also provides perspective. Simply because they've been informed at different levels, those who have a GED or a high school diploma look at an issue one way, while those who have a college education will look at the same issue another way. Both parties have been informed. One has been informed more formally, while the other has been informed more informally.

> **Our attitudes will greatly influence our ability to develop new perspectives.**

6. Then there's the **ancient wisdom** that's embedded in our subconscious, which tells us we can do this, but we shouldn't do that. The Bible's book of Proverbs talks about this. For example, I have been away from my home country of India since 1973, yet there are things from that ancient wisdom that remain part of me.

Once we become aware of the boundaries of our thinking, we can proactively push past these borders to develop new perspectives.

Healthy Attitudes Foster New Perspectives

In addition to knowing how we developed our perspective, we must remain aware of our attitudes. Our attitudes will greatly influence our ability to develop new perspectives.

If we believe that we have to be competent in every area, it breeds an *independent* spirit. While a certain amount of independence is healthy, we must guard against developing a spirit that cannot accept other people's ideas, as this blocks us from gaining new perspective. We have to be healthy enough and free enough to admit that we cannot be strong in every area.

It's much healthier to focus on developing an *interdependent* spirit. As leaders, we don't need to know it all; we just need to know people who have strengths that complement us. We can surround ourselves with people who can show us what we need to see, people who can help us to understand what we need. I don't need to know how to program a computer; I just need someone who can do it for me. I don't need to see everything; I just need to be connected to people who can see what I may not be seeing. You have to be able to select the right advisors, like the president does by picking his cabinet. As I mention in *Who's Holding Your Ladder*, you have to select the right people to hold the ladder that you're climbing.

> **Trans-dependence keeps me rooted in my past, gives me context for my present, and offers me perspective for my future.**

> **Healthy leaders can say, "I don't know everything, I don't need to know everything, and that's not a sign of weakness."**

In the chapter on "New People," I mention the three groups of people that we need to be connected to: Those we are giving a hand up, peers to whom we are reaching out, and people who are where we'd like to be and are reaching down to mentor us. I use the term "*trans-dependence*" to describe how we're related to these three groups of people. We need all three groups to be healthy. Trans-dependence keeps me rooted in my past, gives me context for my present, and offers me perspective for my future.

Healthy leaders can say, "I don't know everything, I don't need to know everything, and that's not a sign of weakness. I only need to be connected to people who can help me achieve my goals."

Research tells us that leaders with the humility to cultivate a healthy, trans-dependent spirit create winning organizations. In his classic study on the characteristics of great leaders, Jim Collins said that an executive with the odd mix of genuine personal humility and an intense professional will was *the* critical component in all high-performing organizations.

> **Instead of saying, "The buck stops here," you're saying, "The buck starts here."**

In defining the traits of these "Level 5 Leaders," Collins says he was shocked by their modesty, by their desire not to talk about themselves but to focus attention on other executives. Collins also found the inverse to be true: Leaders with huge egos are detrimental to their organizations.[10] While their charisma and skills may help make beneficial changes, these leaders weren't able to maintain sustained performance at this level.

Having the humility to go from being the answer person to being a facilitator of your organization's success is a completely different mindset. Instead of saying, "The buck stops here," you're saying, "The buck *starts* here." The leader with perspective gets things started. Once you get things started, you put responsibility in the hands of the right people and *they* stop the buck. You don't know everything and that's not a bad thing. It's just a different perspective.

Connecting People and Perspective

Most often, you'll gain new perspective from other people. When you're trying to figure something out, interacting with people who have other viewpoints fosters new ideas. You'll gain more perspective from other people than you will from attending conferences, reading books, and listening to CDs. When you're searching for new perspective, the place to find it is by connecting with other people.

> **...you have to be comfortable with people who may know more than you.**

But to gain this new perspective, you have to be comfortable with people who may know more than you. That means that you should beware of always being the smartest person in the room. If you're continually traveling in circles where you're the smartest person, that's a sad place to be.

There was a time when people were striving to be the smartest one around. Now, more people realize that they need to be around people who are smarter. They realize that the world they're in is not a stationary landscape, but a dynamic, ever-changing seascape. There's been a shift in thinking and more people are saying, "I need to be around people who know more than me because then I can walk away knowing more than I did when I walked in."

When you're around these smart people, give them sincere permission from your heart to speak into your life. You can say it verbally, but there are other ways to do it. You say it through your actions, you say it by attending talks they may be giving, and you say it by inviting them to lunch. Once you've given them these signals, they won't hesitate to provide input, you won't take it as criticism, and you'll have a new perspective.

> **"I need to be around people who know more than me because then I can walk away knowing more than I did when I walked in."**

Being open to other people's ideas means that we have to be willing to put our own ideas aside. It doesn't work if we have a critical spirit that says, "Well, that works for them but not for me." It also won't work when we have a jealous spirit that says, "I should have thought of that!"

Other people's ideas can only be applied to the degree that we have healthy attitudes. When you're healthy, you don't see other people's ideas as threats; you see them as gifts. When you're healthy, other people's ideas are not just wanted, they're valued and you solicit them. When you're healthy, you call people and ask, "What do you think?"

Healthy leaders know how to solicit other people's ideas. What good is it to ask for someone else's advice and then fight it? If you keep fighting, after a while the person says, "I'm not going to argue with you. You asked me! And now you want me to give you 10 points to corroborate my stance?"

> **When you're healthy, you call people and ask, "What do you think?"**

The most important question that one human being can ask another is,

"What do you think?" There is not a question that respects another person more than that. New perspectives will come when you seek them out, when you ask for them by finding people

> **The most important question that one human being can ask another is, "What do you think?"**

you can ask. Once you ask, you've got an intellectual asset, you're healthy and you have new perspective that you can apply.

Ten Tools for Gaining New Perspective

1. **Ask yourself the Peter Drucker questions:**
   a. What is our mission?
   b. Who is our customer?
   c. What does our customer value?
   d. What is our plan?
   e. What are our results?

2. **Examine and clarify what you offer.** Your product is whatever you offer people. Thinking about this can change your perspective because what you offer changes over time. What I offered a few years ago – running a college – is different from what I offer today, which is life coaching and consultation.

> **The challenge is that you can't show them something that they don't have the capacity to see.**

3. **Offer who you** *are.* What's better: A pastor who gives inspiring sermons or one who gives himself? Certainly, the greatest gift that one human being can give another is to offer themselves. It comes

from focusing on *who you are*, not on *what you do*. Giving myself to my wife is very different from working harder at being a better husband. It's all about emphasizing the inner realities over the external realities. In the end, who we are spills over into what we do.

4. **Recertify yourself each year.** Change is always necessary. We cannot assume that just because something works today, it will continue to work tomorrow. You must either evolve or stagnate.

A leader must continually strive to stay ahead of the game, especially in the area of personal development. While growth and change have been studied for years, they're occurring at a much faster rate than ever recorded in history.

Most leaders only recognize the need for change after decline has set in; they don't take action until something is broken. This is illustrated by point B on Charles Handy's Sigmoid Curve. At that point, the best they can do is put the brakes on to slow it down, begin some crisis management, and put a spin on it.

When you're ahead of the curve and making changes before decline occurs (point A), no one else understands what you're doing or sees why you're doing it. That period between the time that you begin leading a change and the time that others begin seeing what you saw coming is aptly known as *chaos*. When you begin making changes this way, people will tell you, "Why fix it when it's not broken?" The challenge is that you can't show them something that they don't have the capacity to see.

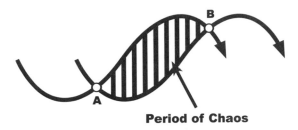

Period of Chaos

Rest assured that you'll experience cycles of chaos. Going from chaos to chaos is how organizations grow, how industries change, and how products evolve. Given that we're always encountering cycles of change, we have to stay ahead of the curve by regularly asking ourselves, "What changes do I need to make?" If we don't, we'll just become part of the landscape. We need to ensure that we're regularly recertifying ourselves by making changes before the need becomes critical.

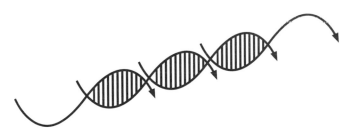

5. **Commit to a personal development plan (PDP).** Many leaders have a personal development plan; they just don't have it written down. For you to develop new perspectives and chart your progress, you should put it in writing. Include what you're going to read, who you're going to be with, things you need to bring into your

life, conferences you'll attend, periodicals you'll subscribe to, and CDs you'll listen to. Then do a quarterly check and hold yourself accountable.

6. **Focus on personal disciplines.** Personal disciplines are *the* determining factor in a leader's success. People all over the world

> **How do you renew yourself?**

ask me, "What do you consider to be *the* make-it-or-break-it issue in leadership?" This is it: personal disciplines. It's not the big stuff that makes or breaks people; it's the small stuff. It's about what time you get up, doing what you say you're going to do, whether you read, and being on time. It's about always telling the truth, treating everybody with respect, and returning phone calls and e-mail.

There are many types of personal disciplines:

- In the area of *handling personal contacts*, for example, I work by a personal discipline known as OHIO, which stands for "Only Handle It Once." When I get e-mail or voicemail, I respond right away so that I don't have to deal with it again. Sometimes, I'll forward the message and ask my assistant to follow up. If I need to respond to an e-mail that's fairly extensive, I reply with a short message saying that I got the message, that I will think about the matter, and then get back to the person. Then I follow through; it's a matter of personal discipline for me.

- *Reading widely.* I always encourage people to read outside the narrow sphere of their interests, to read about the areas that they want to be in, not the ones they're in right now. I read as much secular literature as I do sacred literature. I read a magazine called *Fast Company*, I read *Leader to Leader*, Peter Drucker, the *Harvard Business Review*. I read all the way from leadership light to leadership heavy.

- *Growing intentionally.* When Bob Dylan wrote, "He not busy being born is busy dying," he was saying that people need to make sure that they're always renewing themselves. How do you renew yourself? For me, I'm always finding new people to be around. Given my work, that's not a difficult thing to do. I'm always looking for new things to read, and looking for people who can give me new perspective. I have a plan to keep growing.

> **"In times of change, learners inherit the earth, while the learned find themselves beautifully equipped to deal with a world that no longer exists."**

7. **Remember that the learners beat the learned.** Eric Hoffer emphasized the importance of learning quite well when he wrote, "In times of change, learners inherit the earth, while the learned find themselves beautifully equipped to deal with a world that no longer exists." Somebody with a Ph.D. who has not continued growing is learned. A person with a GED who is a learner, who continues growing and developing, can outdistance that Ph.D. I may have a graduate degree in computer science, but if I don't keep up with my field, I'm learned. Unless I'm an active learner, it's just a degree that looks good on my resume.

8. **Be content to be "a work in progress."** I'm not where I was yesterday; I'm not where I'm going to be tomorrow. I'm in progress. That's a very healthy perspective. It means that if you correct me on something today, I won't take umbrage. I will just regard it as part of the growth process.

9. **Remember, it's not the destination; it's the journey.** Have you ever heard children on a long trip saying, "Are we there yet?" Their parents patiently encourage them to find ways to enjoy the journey. What about us? Are *we* enjoying the trip? Are we having fun yet or are we obsessed with our destination? When I have perspective, I know that I don't have to have it all together, I don't always have to have all the answers because I'm a work in progress. When I make a mistake, it's not because I did something wrong. It's simply that I wasn't there in that part of the process.

> **There are no mistakes if you've learned something in the process.**

10. **Ask yourself three questions at the end of every day:**

   • What did I learn today? What spoke both to your heart and your head?

   • How did I grow today? What touched your heart and affected your actions?

   • What will I do differently? Unless you can tell me what you plan to do differently, you didn't learn anything. There are no mistakes if you've learned something in the process.

If I were to call you at the end of the day, what would you answer? These three questions not only give you something to add to your personal development plan daily, but by making them part of your PDP you'll be nurturing the on-going growth of new perspectives in your life.

Gaining new perspectives is not something that's just going to happen to you; they won't fall out of the sky. You have to make it happen by creating the right conditions and putting yourself in situations that will lead to growth. By regularly working with these tools, you'll put yourself on the right road – the road to new perspectives.

Teaching Points

- New perspectives provide value in the business world and growth within organizations.

- Gaining new perspective involves forcing ourselves to think in new ways.

- To gain new perspective, we should be aware of the six primary origins of our current perspective: family, friends, foes, culture, education, and ancient wisdom.

  - Family provides our core values, our history, prejudices, fears, biases and preferences.

  - Interacting with our friends brings us the influence of their families.

  - As we "keep our friends close and our enemies closer," our foes help us develop new perspective.

  - The influence of our part of the world also offers us perspective.

  - Education provides perspective by offering other ways to think about issues.

  - We also gain perspective from the ancient wisdom embedded in our subconscious.

- Becoming aware of the borders of our thinking helps us to proactively push into new perspective.

- Healthy attitudes influence our ability to develop new perspective.

- Rather than developing an independent spirit that tries to be strong in every area, leaders should focus on being interdependent by surrounding themselves with others who have complementary strengths.

- To be healthy, leaders need to be trans-dependent by being connected to those they are giving a hand up, peers they are reaching out to, and people they are reaching up to for mentoring.

- Research shows that leaders with a mix of personal humility and intense professional will are the critical component in all high-performing organizations.

- When you're searching for new perspective, the place to find it is by connecting with other people.

- Healthy leaders value and solicit the perspectives of other people.

- Regularly working with these ten tools can help you gain new perspective:

  - Ask yourself the Drucker questions:

    - What is our mission?

    - Who is our customer?

    - What does our customer value?

    - What is our plan?

    - What are our results?

  - Regularly evaluate what you offer, as what you offer can change over time.

  - Offer who you are, not what you do.

  - Going from chaos to chaos is how organizations grow. Stay ahead of changes by recertifying your offerings annually.

  - Commit to a written personal development plan (PDP).

- Personal disciplines – such as handling personal contacts, reading widely, and growing intentionally – are *the* determining factor in a leader's success.

- Remember that the learners beat the learned.

- There are no mistakes if you've learned something in the process.

- Be content to be a work in progress.

- At the end of every day, focus on what you learned, how you grew and what you'll do differently.

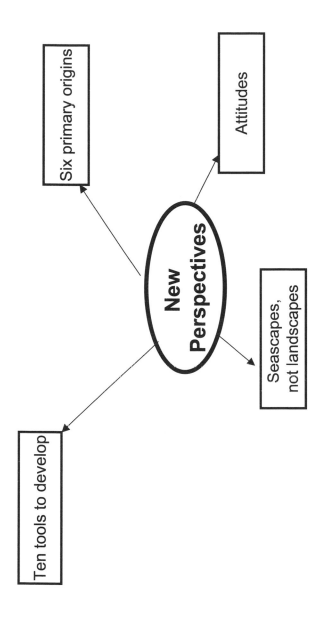

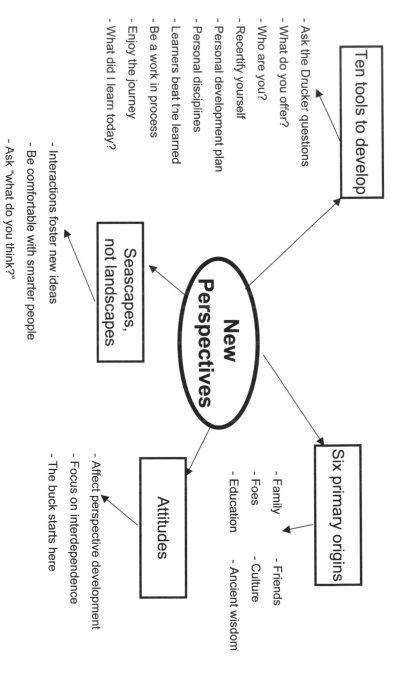

New Perspectives

Ten tools to develop
- Ask the Drucker questions
- What do you offer?
- Who are you?
- Recertify yourself
- Personal development plan
- Personal disciplines
- Learners beat the learned
- Be a work in process
- Enjoy the journey
- What did I learn today?

Seascapes, not landscapes
- Interactions foster new ideas
- Be comfortable with smarter people
- Ask "what do you think?"

Six primary origins
- Family   - Friends
- Foes   - Culture
- Education   - Ancient wisdom

Attitudes
- Affect perspective development
- Focus on interdependence
- The buck starts here

5

New Priorities

There is surely nothing quite so useless as doing with great efficiency what should not be done at all[11].

– Peter F. Drucker, Business Analyst/Author

Sitting in his garage workshop, watching the wood shavings falling from the edge of his knife, Paul felt himself relax. As he did, his thoughts turned to the issues facing his software company.

Despite its financial success, Paul instinctively felt that the company was doing too many things. After their early success in creating graphics for computer games, they expanded into animation sequences for Web sites and software programs. They'd even launched their own computer game, which achieved some industry recognition.

Paul wondered how these activities were connected with the company's vision, which was to be the graphics provider of choice for the computer-game industry. He'd always assumed that diversifying was beneficial, since it brought revenue from different areas. Staring at the chisel in his hand, Paul knew that honing his woodcarving tools to a fine edge was what improved their performance. He wondered what adjustments he could make to gain the same focused effort from his organization.

I f you're a Baby Boomer like me, you're probably thinking about downsizing your life. Our generation is examining our experiences and distilling our lives into the essentials. No one wants to be working as hard in their sixties as they did in their forties. But everyone does want to have a bigger impact at sixty than they did at forty. To make that happen, your activity must be focused; it must be honed to a fine edge.

Leaders at this stage of life might focus their efforts in different ways. A pastor might stop pastoring full-time, for example, and use his pastoral-care expertise as a consultant to other churches. Depending on her background, she could become part of a stewardship company and raise money for churches. I, for example, limit my focus to one thing: leadership. I use three delivery

> **Whenever your organization focuses on a few essential priorities, it gains strength.**

systems – consultations, conferences, and resources, including books, and CD's – but everything I do is about equipping leaders. That's my priority.

Focusing on priorities is good for organizations too. Whenever your organization focuses on a few essential priorities, it gains strength. Peter Drucker described organizations as purposefully designed tools created for specialized tasks. The more specialized their task, the greater their strength. Diversifying destroys an organization's capacity to perform, said Drucker. It's an effective organization only when it's narrowly focused.

Finding your essential priorities gives you momentum and provides energy. The Apostle Paul understood the power of the essential few when he wrote, "This one thing I do[12]." He also knew that his priority was preaching to the Gentiles, just as the Apostle Peter's priority was preaching to the Jews.

The power of focusing on a few essential priorities is something most of us are familiar with. For example, if I was visiting your town and we decided to have a good steak dinner, where would you take me? Chances are that you wouldn't think of taking me to a Shoney's, a Denny's, or the local diner. When you were planning that steak dinner, you probably thought of a steak house, a place that only focuses on an essential few. You weren't thinking about going somewhere that serves breakfast anytime, where you can order liver and onions, spaghetti, and anything else you want. You intuitively recognized that the better you are, the fewer things you do.

> ...your vision is the source of your priorities.

Fulfilling your vision requires you to be focused on a few essential priorities. You have to work smarter, not harder. Gaining that critical focus involves answering three important questions:

- What are my priorities?

- How should I implement these priorities?

- How can I effectively communicate my priorities within my organization?

Finding the Essential Few

To define your priorities, start by examining your vision. Your vision and your priorities will always be inextricably linked. That's because your vision is the source of your priorities. When you want to define your priorities, your vision provides you with the necessary context.

For example, my own vision is empowering leaders. My Web site explains that my vision is creating a leadership culture, helping others to succeed, having leaders producing other leaders. That vision provides a context for what my priorities should be and what they should *not* be. My priorities should not be focused on praise and worship, on theology, or on church growth. They should revolve around leadership. That doesn't mean that I won't have influence in those areas. There will always be some overlap, but my primary focus is leadership.

When your vision provides the context for your priorities, it becomes much easier to make choices. To illustrate, let's say that I have two opportunities available to me. Both opportunities are on the same day, so I can't take both. I have to decide whether I will preach to a stadium crowd of 10,000 people or meet with

> **...every decision and every business activity is headed for obsolescence the minute it begins.**

100 leaders about leadership development. I don't even have to think about it; my mind is already made up. Because my vision provides me with context, you'll find me in a room with those 100 leaders.

Don't make the mistake of thinking that once you've established your priorities that they're forever carved in stone, however. Peter Drucker said that every product, every decision and every business activity is headed for obsolescence the minute it begins. We can blame it on market shifts, on cultural pressures, or on the third law of thermodynamics, but it's inevitable.

Effective leaders are constantly re-evaluating their priorities, regularly putting them on trial to ensure that they're focusing on the right activities. As mentioned in the chapter on "New Perspectives," we cannot assume that just because something works today, it will continue to work tomorrow. It's important to ensure that what was important yesterday is still important today. You can't wait for situations to decline before you evaluate your priorities; you have to stay ahead of the game. You do that by remaining aware of the environment you're operating in and continually evaluating your priorities.

Obviously, your priorities should affect how you invest your time. It's important that you ensure that you're making the most of your time by scheduling your priorities rather than prioritizing your schedule. What's the difference? When you're prioritizing your schedule, you're simply looking at the schedule you already have and ranking what's most important. But

> **Ensure that you're making the most of your time by scheduling your priorities rather than prioritizing your schedule.**

when you schedule your priorities, you're starting by allocating time to your priorities. That ensures that you're devoting the necessary time to what's important to you. They're two different ways of looking at things, but only one approach helps you to achieve your vision.

Putting Your Priorities to Work

Once you've determined your priorities, it's important to develop a strategic plan to implement them. Doing this ensures that your priorities mesh with your organization's vision. For example, if you were developing priorities for the Ritz-Carlton, each priority should reflect their vision for providing stellar customer service to their guests.

Developing a plan to implement your priorities involves answering a number of questions:

- How does this priority support our vision?

- In what specific ways can we implement this priority?

- Who will be responsible for these activities?

- What's the timeframe for accomplishing this priority?

- Do we have the capacity to undertake this right now? Do we have the necessary finances, people and facilities?

- How will we measure success?

Your answers to these questions will ensure that your vision, mission, values and priorities are properly aligned. My book, *What's Shaking Your Ladder*, describes this alignment as *organizational congruence*. Having organizational congruence provides energy, focus and passion. You'll know where you're going, where you're *not* going, how you'll get there, and how you'll know that you've arrived.

Whenever you implement new priorities, you also have to deal with a variety of implementation obstacles. It would be great if you could instantly adopt, plan and execute new priorities, but that rarely happens.

Having organizational congruence provides energy, focus and passion.

Organizations are made up of people, and people cannot handle instant change. They need time to make the transition to the organization's new priorities. Because of this, if you want to successfully implement new priorities, you have to help people make the necessary emotional, relational, and psychological changes.

It's not always wise or always possible to completely disengage from old priorities when new ones emerge. For example, if your new priority involves entering a new market or providing a new service, you might not want to – or be able to – discard your other products and other markets. Your staff may have emotional ties to products and services to which they've grown accustomed. They also may be wrestling with fear about the chances for success in a new market. For those and many other reasons, it's best to plan your transitions.

When I was preparing to resign as president of Beulah Heights Bible College, I spent a lot of time in transition planning. I met with the board members individually, explained what I was going to do and why, consulted with high-impact leaders who had made significant transitions themselves, and developed a successor. I couldn't immediately disengage from my old priorities; I had to prepare a transition plan. I had to disengage from the old priorities without discarding them while also being sure that I was moving forward with my new priorities.

Another common problem in implementing priorities is protecting yourself from well-intentioned people who want to impose other priorities on you. Since people always have helpful suggestions to make, you have to be sold on your priorities and be diplomatic in dealing with distractions.

Your priorities must be birthed by your vision.

Rick Warren says that he's always meeting people who think that Saddleback Church should adopt practices from their last church. They tell him, "At our old church, we did it like this…" He says he finds himself wondering how he can politely inform them that Saddleback has its own vision. Rick Warren understands the importance of staying true to his God-given vision and priorities.

Now that's not to say that people won't provide valuable suggestions that could be useful in the future. You don't want to discourage input. You just have to ensure that what you do fits with your vision, doesn't overextend your resources, and is not imposed on you. Your priorities must be birthed by your vision.

When you know your destiny, your purpose and your God-given priorities, you know what you're built to do. And that makes it easier to stay focused and not let other people – however well intentioned they are – set your priorities.

Communicating Priorities to Others

If you want people to get behind the organization's priorities and make them their own, you first have to sell them on your vision. A noted expert on change and transition, William Bridges, says that people won't understand the solution you're proposing (your vision and priorities) until they understand the problem. It's a leader's job to provide them with the guidance and the information they need to understand what needs to happen and why.

Getting people engaged with a vision and priorities involves more than making an announcement or holding a meeting or two and expecting them to get it. You have to communicate persuasively; you have to sell them on the vision just like you're speaking with investors. You have to cast your vision, like you'd cast a line to get a fish.

> **...people won't understand the solution you're proposing until they understand the problem.**

Getting people engaged with a vision and priorities is an art known as *vision casting*.

Effective vision casting involves following a few principles:

- **Keep it simple.** Articulate the vision and priorities in terms that people understand. Keep it as simple as possible. The simpler the better. Use short sentences and short words. You're really aiming at making it digestible.

- **Make it memorable.** Work at making the vision easy to remember. My vision, for example, is "*Helping others succeed.*" Your vision should be short enough to fit on a tee shirt. If it doesn't fit, it's too long and people won't remember it.

- **Have a stable vision.** Over time, your vision and priorities will expand. But the essence shouldn't change dramatically. If you're continually making significant changes to your vision, it changes the organization too much and confuses people.

- **Be patient.** Most important, give people time to catch on. When you have new priorities, you have to allow people time to engage with them. Remember that by the time we unveil new priorities to the organization, we've been living with them for quite some time. We've had time to engage with them and make them part of us. Too many leaders make the mistake of thinking that people should get the priorities after a few staff meetings. It doesn't work that quickly. Your people are just beginning their own journey with the new priorities. Be patient with them and always find ways to help them to become engaged with the priorities and the vision.

If you want an example of an organization that's realizing the benefit of having people engaged with a vision and its priorities, look at the Web retailer Amazon.com. Their vision centers on creating the world's most customer-centered company, where people can find and buy anything online.

One of Amazon's priorities, according to CEO Jeff Bezos, is conserving money for things that matter[13]. All of their desks – even the ones used by their executives – are modeled after the one Bezos built for himself from a door, some metal brackets and sawed two-by-fours when he started the company. That's one creative way to communicate a priority!

Some of the things that Amazon does seems like they'd lead to decreased sales. If you've ever visited their Web site, you know that people post online reviews of products that Amazon sells. In some cases, the reviews can be pretty negative. Bezos says that when they started doing this, people told him he didn't understand much about business. In his mind, however, enabling people to post online reviews is fulfilling Amazon's vision because it assists customers in making purchasing decisions.

Did you know that Amazon even warns customers when they're about to purchase a CD that they previously purchased from the site? For many companies, that might seem like another example of poor business sense. To Amazon, it's implementing one of the essential priorities of their customer-centered vision.

Like Amazon, you can find strength by recognizing the priorities that are aligned with your vision, focusing on those few essential priorities, and becoming the best by focusing your energy on only a few things.

Teaching Points

- Priorities offer a bigger impact from more focused effort.

- A focused organization gains strength, while diversifying destroys its capacity to perform.

- The better you are, the fewer things you do.

- Gaining focus comes from asking: what are my priorities, how should I implement my priorities and how can I effectively communicate within my organization?

- To discover your priorities, start by examining your vision, which provides context for your priorities, in addition to being their source.

- The context provided by your priorities makes it easier to make choices.

- Re-evaluate your priorities regularly to ensure proper focus, rather than waiting for situations to decline.

- Schedule your priorities; don't prioritize your schedule. Devote time to what's important.

- Develop a plan to implement your priorities by asking:

  - How does this priority support our vision?

  - In what specific ways can we implement this priority?

  - Who will be responsible for these activities?

  - What's the timeframe for accomplishing this priority?

  - Do we have the capacity to undertake this right now? Do we have the necessary finances, people and facilities?

  - How will we measure success?

- Organizational congruence occurs when there is alignment between your vision, values and priorities.

- You must help people in your organization to make the emotional, relational, and psychological changes that are part of the transition to new priorities.

- It's not always wise or practical to completely disengage from old priorities. Instead, you must plan transitions.

- Guard against others imposing their priorities on you.

- When communicating priorities, remember that you must sell people in a way that helps them to understand the problem and the solution you're proposing.

- When casting your vision, keep it simple, memorable and stable. And be patient.

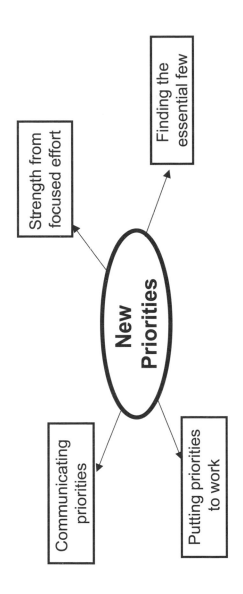

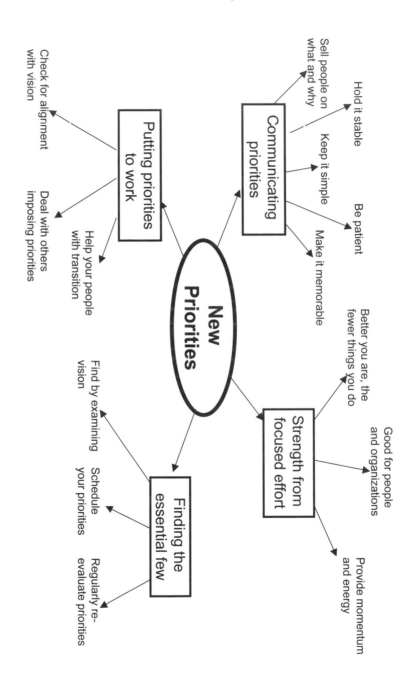

6

New Passions

"There is a time for everything, and a season for every activity under heaven.

– Ecclesiastes 3:1

He wasn't really sick. Jake just couldn't face another day of lengthy meetings, phone calls and planning sessions. Driving to the golf course, he had begun feeling guilty, thinking that he was behaving less like the senior pastor of a growing church and more like a student cutting classes.

If this had been the only day he'd played hooky, he might have felt differently. But Jake's need for unscheduled time off, his lengthy periods of daydreaming, and his loss of focus were beginning to concern him. Despite a two-week vacation, he noticed that he was still just as edgy and restless. Was it burn out? A mid-life crisis?

Pulling his golf clubs from the trunk of the car, Jake set the bag down and stared at the clubhouse with his hands in his pockets. He'd always thought that counseling was for weaker souls without goals or purpose. Was he wrong? Lost in his thoughts, he didn't hear or notice the valet until he tugged gently on Jake's sleeve.

It might be hard for you to imagine this now, especially if you're in the early stages of realizing your vision. But, as your journey continues, you may discover that the dreams and the visions that once compelled you are beginning to lose their intensity. In fact, they might someday become routine, even boring.

You might shake your head at this suggestion. You cannot imagine yourself feeling less fulfilled, let alone feeling bored by what you're doing. But it happens. When it does, it's important for you to remember that it's an entirely natural occurrence. Or maybe you're experiencing this shift right now, saying, "Yes, that's me."

When my own vision began to lose its luster, I wasn't quite sure what was causing the problem. I responded by making myself busier, diving in with renewed commitment to my duties as president of Beulah Heights Bible College. As hard as I tried, the boredom, the feelings that I had done all of this before, the sense that there were no new mountains to climb did not go away. I thought that there was something wrong with me. It took a while to learn that what I was experiencing was quite normal.

It's typical for visionary leaders to become uncomfortable with the status quo.

No leader – not even Bill Gates – is exempt from these changes in passion. When Gates started Microsoft, you'd hear his passion about his work whenever he spoke. Talk with him today, however, and you might be surprised to find that his passion has shifted. That's exactly what one writer for *New York* magazine discovered while listening to Gates speak not long after he stepped down as Microsoft CEO to run the Gates Foundation.

"It was clear to all in the auditorium that software no longer got Gates' juices pumping the way his work at the foundation did," the article says. "Technology questions were answered quickly, without passion, whereas questions about global health elicited lengthy disquisitions full of detail and emotion. The way he talked about wiping out malaria was how he used to talk about wiping out Netscape.[14]" Now that's a change in passion!

It's typical for visionary leaders to become uncomfortable with the status quo. People with this particular talent may be exemplary leaders when they're in the position of reviving a dying company or launching a brand new effort. They're just not the same ones equipped to run its daily operations for an extended period. Put a gifted visionary in an operating environment for too long and they become restless, bored, and ready for another challenge.

Peter Cuneo, currently the vice chairman, former president and CEO of Marvel Entertainment, describes the limits of this talent quite well. "We turnaround types are often the wrong person to lead a well-oiled machine. Typically I stay for three or four years and then move on.[15]" No wonder Cuneo is well known for performing successful turnarounds

> **Put a gifted visionary in an operating environment for too long and they become restless, bored, and ready for another challenge.**

at seven consumer-product companies, including Clairol, Black & Decker, Remington and Marvel. He's aware of his particular gift and listens to the inner voice of his own passion.

Remember: There's nothing wrong with the visionary leader who doesn't get excited when they've gone as far as their gift permits, who wants to move on once the company is performing well. The trick is knowing when it's happening to you. As the song puts it, you have to "know when to hold `em, know when to fold `em."

Navigating Changing Passions

Legends about Alexander the Great say that when he realized that he had conquered the entire known world, he sat down and cried because there were no more mountains for him to climb. Maybe that's what you're feeling.

It's similar to what happened to me. As I describe in my book, *Who Moved Your Ladder?*, I awoke early one morning, thought through my schedule for the day and wanted to call in sick. I'd worked very hard to make the college successful, to create the events that filled my calendar every day, but there I was fighting boredom and restlessness. It was a difficult time.

> **...visionaries have to learn to slow down and listen to ourselves.**

During the months I spent navigating my changing passions, I learned some truths that might help you in your own journey. Navigating changing passions is easier when you can:

- Admit when things have changed
- Look for godly discontent
- Leave on a high note

Admit when things have changed. This sounds too simple to even state. However, visionaries have to learn to slow down and listen to ourselves. That isn't always easy for us. My path through the problem of changing passions began when I could admit that *I was having a problem.* It wasn't the school that was the problem; the problem was Sam Chand! I had to admit that I was drifting, that I was bored, that the things that used to excite me didn't do so any longer. It had become a routine, something I felt I could do in my sleep.

Many leaders have a hard time admitting such things, especially if they're visionaries. We don't want to see ourselves drifting with the current or standing still. We tell ourselves that we're tired, burned out, or need to get away and recharge our batteries. We always want to be going somewhere, so we get busier and think that's enough. But activity isn't always progress.

...activity isn't always progress.

Don't avoid taking time to analyze what's going on inside you; continued neglect of your feelings can have negative repercussions. It can drive you into a funk or a depression, which will have an effect on your decision-making ability, as well as your relationships.

Take some time and listen to yourself. If you discover that you're bored, pay attention to those feelings. You might just find that you're caught between where you are and where you could be tomorrow.

Look for godly discontent. It's easy to identify when something is *not* godly discontent. For example, some leaders move to avoid dealing with problems. While that's not godly discontent, it is human nature. It's also the reason that I always advise leaders to avoid making any high-level transitions before checking the internal health of their organization. You always want to be sure that you're not avoiding working through some difficult issues.

Others confuse their feelings of restlessness with the effects of the Peter Principle. Because they've risen to the level of their incompetence, they know they can't do an adequate job. Moving on isn't the answer because they're only avoiding dealing with issues of their own personal growth. If they lack a competency in a certain area or an inability to relate to certain types of people, it will follow them wherever they go if they don't deal with it.

On the other hand, godly discontent wants to produce the best for yourself and for your organization. If you decide to move on, no one will be shortchanged. If you stay, it will create growth for you and for the organization. Godly discontent is the first step in disengaging from the old challenges to be prepared for new ones.

Leave on a high note. When I left the college, I could say that I met each goal and challenge that confronted me. I left on a high note by communicating my intent to the board, by preparing a successor to ensure the continued success of the organization, as well as by maintaining a positive attitude.

There's nothing to gain by burning your bridges when you go. You never know when you'll need something from your former organization.

> **...what do you do when one passion is growing while another is decreasing?**

Don't use your final days to vent your anger or dissatisfaction. Resolve those issues before you depart. Leave with a smile on your face. Choosing to move on is always a difficult decision. Venting negative feelings just makes it more difficult for everyone.

Regardless of how challenging it might be, remain focused on the positive. While I'm an optimistic person, I found more faults in my last few months at the college than in all previous 14 years combined. I had to question why this was happening. I concluded that it was because I was in the process of disengaging and unconsciously needed to convince myself that I was making the right decision. I kept telling myself that I wasn't leaving because something was wrong, but because I was taking the next step in my own life.

Uncovering New Passions

There's a lot written for people coping with being fired or laid off. But there's not much to tell you how to cope with these disturbing feelings when you're doing well, when you're successful, when you've achieved more than you've ever dreamed. When I began my search for resources to assist me through my transition, I found little that helped me deal with my decisions and my issues.

For example, how do you discover the next ladder that you want to climb? And what do you do when one passion is growing while another is decreasing? These times of transition are not comfortable. Once you realize that you're in the midst of a transition and that you lack maps of this new territory, you can begin to make peace.

When *Fast Company* profiled people who were transitioning between long-term corporate jobs and their own businesses, they said that "Corporate dropouts concede that one of the most difficult things is to maintain the same level of enthusiasm for the job you're about to leave as the venture you're about to start.[16]"

In my case, my passion for consulting was increasing while my passion for leading the college was decreasing. This disturbed my equilibrium. During this time of transition, I was keeping both irons in the fire for a while. I just had to make peace with those facts and give both my very best efforts.

Uncovering a new passion is another challenge. Some leaders find their passion in less-than-ideal circumstances. When Steve Case was forced out after the Time Warner-AOL merger, he launched a company that focused on providing consumer-friendly health-care services. The idea was inspired partly by his brother's brain cancer diagnosis and his own frustrations with finding a doctor when a child was sick on the weekend.

Discerning your own passion may not be evident that quickly. You may have to search for it. This requires a great deal of soul searching, trusting your instincts, and honestly asking yourself many hard questions. Uncovering your passion involves two major things:

- Finding your path

- Staying on course

Finding your path involves thinking about your core values and dreams. This might be uncomfortable at first because many leaders become used to dealing with hard results, while these deliberations are more concerned with softer issues.

You have to come up with your own answers to questions, such as:

- What do I really care about?

- What makes me pound the table with passion?

- What do I dream about?

- Where do I get my greatest fulfillment?

- When I daydream, what values are at work?

- What have I liked most about what I've done?

Once you think you've found your passion, ask if you're passionate enough about what you're considering to stay at it for the rest of your professional career. If it's only temporary, what are your motives for moving in that direction? If you are passionate about it, that's a good indication that you're headed down the right path.

Staying on course requires getting some help. People don't realize their passions for a few common reasons. Sometimes, they lack a clearly defined objective. Other times, it's because they have no method to keep themselves motivated or they do not devote time to their passion.

You may not have a clear picture of your passion, but you can take a single step toward making it clearer with this short exercise. Make a copy of the next page of this book, complete the questions and ask someone to make you accountable for taking that small step. If you didn't take that step, that's fine. Just commit to another date for getting it done.

> **The jump is so frightening between where I am and where I could be...Because of all I may become, I will close my eyes and leap!**

Once you do this, you can then commit to taking another small step for another date. By doing this, you're getting support from someone else in realizing your dream and you're connecting the many small steps it will take to realize that big dream. These are two additional reasons that keep people from realizing their dreams.

Once I knew where I had to go, where my passion was leading me, I became alive again. Once you find yourself headed in the right direction, your own passion will return.

The jump is so frightening between where I am and where I could be...Because of all I may become, I will close my eyes and leap![17]

Steps to Uncovering Your Passion

1. Write down the *short version* of your dream.

    _____

    _____

    _____

    _____

    _____

2. Write down the *first step* you must take to fulfill your dream.

    _____

    _____

    _____

    _____

    _____

3. Commit to a *date* when you'll have completed the first step.

    _____

    _____

    _____

    _____

    _____

4. Give someone a copy of this sheet and your phone number today. Ask them to call you on the date you wrote down to see if you've taken the first step.

    _____

    _____

    _____

    _____

    _____

5. If you took the step, use another copy of the sheet to commit to the next small step.

    _____

    _____

    _____

    _____

    _____

6. If no step was taken, give the person another date and ask them to call again.

    _____

    _____

    _____

    _____

    _____

Teaching Points

- Our passions shift at various stages of life. It's perfectly normal for something that was once a passionate pursuit to become a mere interest.

- No leader is exempt from these changes in passion.

- Put a gifted visionary in an operating environment for too long and they become restless, bored, and ready for another challenge.

- There's nothing wrong with the visionary leader who doesn't get excited and wants to move on once a company is performing well.

- Navigating changing passions is easier when you can admit when things have changed, look for godly discontent, and leave on a high note.

- Many leaders have a hard time admitting they're even having a problem. Take some time and pay attention to your feelings.

- Look for the godly discontent that may be preparing you for new challenges. This discontent wants the best for you and for the organization.

- You can leave on a high note by remaining focused on this positive fact: that you're leaving to take the next step in your life.

- There's little guidance for leaders in times of transition, who have these disturbing feelings when they've achieved more than they've ever dreamed.

- Uncovering a new passion is challenging. It requires a great deal of soul searching, trusting your instincts, and honestly asking yourself many hard questions.

- Uncovering your passion involves finding your path and staying on course.

  - Finding your path involves thinking about your core values and dreams, which is thinking about softer issues.

  - If you think you can stay at what you're considering for the rest of your professional career, you may be headed down the right path.

- People don't realize their passions because they lack a clearly defined objective, they have no method to keep themselves motivated, or they do not devote time to their passion.

- Staying on course involves getting help from someone in realizing your dream. Make yourself accountable to take the next step.

- By getting help and connecting the many small steps it takes to realize your big dream, you overcome two additional issues that keep people from realizing their dreams.

- Once you find yourself headed in the right direction, your own passion will return.

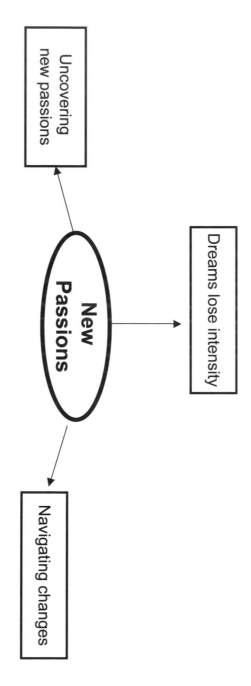

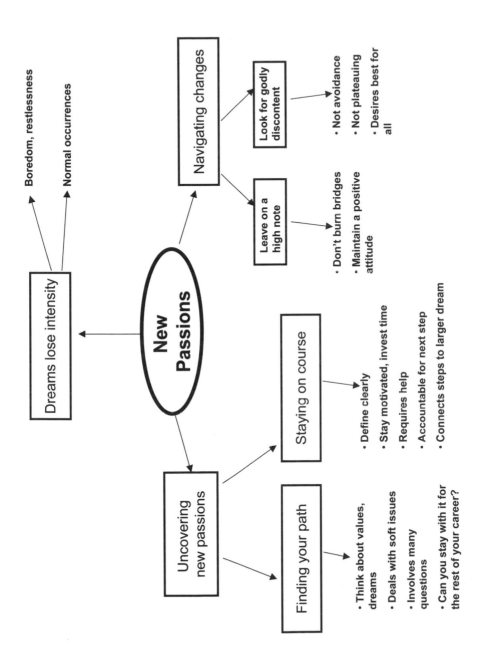

New Passions

Dreams lose intensity
- Boredom, restlessness
- Normal occurrences

Navigating changes
- Look for godly discontent
  - Not avoidance
  - Not plateauing
  - Desires best for all
- Leave on a high note
  - Don't burn bridges
  - Maintain a positive attitude

Uncovering new passions
- Staying on course
  - Define clearly
  - Stay motivated, invest time
  - Requires help
  - Accountable for next step
  - Connects steps to larger dream
- Finding your path
  - Think about values, dreams
  - Deals with soft issues
  - Involves many questions
  - Can you stay with it for the rest of your career?

7

New Preparation

Forewarned is forearmed. To be prepared is half the victory.

– Spanish Proverb

Disturbed by a conversation he couldn't get out of his head, Pastor Jake Barrett was making little progress on his sermon. Earlier that day, he called a friend pastoring in another state, only to find the man wrestling with concerns over the upcoming closing of a nearby military base, an event that would cause more than half the families in the church to relocate. Jake listened as the shocked pastor talked about the effect this loss would have on the church's building program, its Christian school, and to his questions about the church's future.

Browsing through his membership roster, Jake wondered what effect a similar occurrence would have on his own congregation. How prepared would they be if one or more of the area's largest employers decided to consolidate facilities in a less-expensive state? What about more immediate concerns? Was he preparing future deacons and Sunday school teachers to replace those who might leave the area when the current people retired? Looking at the calendar on his desk, he wondered how he could possibly equip himself to deal with whatever tomorrow might bring.

W̲e live in an era where we control very little. For leaders who value planning, this can be especially trying. Not long ago, someone could develop a strategic plan, create the associated processes, and be fairly confident of the outcome. Now, because of the accelerated rate of change, we must do more than plan. We must invest time in preparation.

Many leaders don't understand the difference between planning and preparation. They make the mistake of thinking of them as synonymous, when they're not. Planning has a narrow focus, while preparation is far broader in its scope. When you *prepare*, you're readying

> **...we must do more than plan. We must invest time in preparation.**

yourself in advance, you're priming yourself, getting warmed up for any possibility. When you *plan*, you're devising a method to achieve some specific end.

For example, if you felt led into ministry, you probably *prepared* yourself by attending Bible school or seminary. You took classes in Greek and Hebrew, studied the New Testament and the Old Testament to ready yourself for what you would do. Let's say that you thought you'd become a pastor, but you really weren't sure. One day, you heard a presentation about the work being done by a specific organization. You realized immediately that was what you were called to do; it fit you in so many ways. Now that you know what you want to do – work with that organization – you began making specific *plans* by taking certain courses and investigating what that organization looks for in people they work with.

There is certainly a time for planning. But we cannot overlook the importance of preparation. Proverbs reminds us, "The mind of man plans his way, but the Lord directs his steps[18]." In the end, we have to be ready for our steps to be directed, even if that means going somewhere that's contrary to our original plans. We simply have to be prepared for whatever comes our way.

> **I know too many organizations whose realities have changed, but they are still following the strategic plan associated with a landscape.**

The environment that we work in, the industries in which our businesses compete, and the entire world we live in are changing rapidly. We cannot assume that today's conditions will remain true tomorrow. All too quickly, the landscape we're standing on becomes a raging seascape. If we're going to successfully surf that seascape, we have to be prepared.

I know too many organizations whose realities have changed, but they are still following the strategic plan associated with a landscape. That's the result of inadequate preparation on many levels. Rather than articulate our strategic plans with a landscape perspective, we must adopt both the outlook and the language of the seascape.

Becoming a Prepared Leader

How can we prepare for what lies ahead? How do we prepare ourselves for the inevitable changes we'll confront? How can we best prepare the organizations that we serve?

We have to make preparations on various levels. Like a doctor conducting routine physicals, we must regularly inquire about several areas:

- *Personal preparation.* We have to examine the effect that our character, our personality issues, and our hang-ups might have on our future effectiveness. For example, if you're in sales, you'll never excel until you become adept at the art of chitchat. You have to be comfortable making small talk. "Hey, how are you? Tell me about your family. How are you doing?" If you're the type of person who wants to get right to the point and sell your widget, you're going to be less effective than someone who can establish rapport. Regardless of what field you're in, you have to spend time thinking about what character-related adjustments can help you to be more personally prepared.

> **There is simply no substitute for being professionally prepared.**

- *Professional preparation.* We also have to be prepared in whatever our area of competency happens to be. We have to always stay ahead of the curve. If you work with computers, for example, you'll want to be current with the latest hardware and software. If you're a tax accountant, you have to be fluent with the upcoming and most recent changes in the laws. We also should get whatever certifications that we, or our organization, might need. There is simply no substitute for being professionally prepared.

- *Relational preparation.* It's important to be aware of our chemistry, which is how we get along with people. How comfortable are we when we meet new people? Are there certain types of people that we find difficult to work with? How well do we manage and negotiate conflict? In the end, if we don't click relationally with someone, we may find ourselves limited. That's why it's important to be prepared relationally.

- *Family preparation.* We simply cannot ignore the importance of preparing our family. Sometimes, the preparation can be fairly simply. For example, my children needed to understand what work I was going to do when I left my role at the college. I didn't want them wondering what their dad does. Sometimes, the preparation might be more complex, such as when you have to relocate. Since we're not the only ones who

> **We simply cannot ignore the importance of preparing our family.**

are affected, our families have to be prepared. They have to be prepared for the new priorities, the new places, and the new pains that they'll face.

- *Financial preparation.* When I was at the college, I was very well paid. Since I was going to be self-employed, I had to be ready for no regular paycheck, no benefits, and no paid vacation. My wife and I prepared by talking about how to arrange our finances. We asked ourselves, "What expenses could we downsize?" If you're looking at changes in your organization, you may have to go through a similar process with your accountant. Even if you don't have the information you need for detailed planning, you can make financial preparations for what might be coming.

- *Educational preparation.* There are many people working in areas where they have no formal education. It's rare that you find someone working in the same discipline that they majored in when they were in college. I don't have any formal training in the specific area I am working in now. In some ways, I feel like a trail-blazing pioneer. That means that I

> **Opportunities come to those who are prepared.**

have had to constantly educate myself through the many avenues available to me, including industry associations, seminars, magazines, and books. I have to continually make sure that I'm preparing myself educationally for what lies ahead.

Rewards of Preparation

Let's face it – despite our research, our strategies and our plans, many things can happen that we haven't planned on. While we may not control these events, we do control how prepared we are. Leaders who are prepared can make a world of difference.

Opportunities come to those who are prepared. When we're

> **The opportunity of a lifetime must be utilized in the lifetime of the opportunity.**

prepared, we'll recognize the right opportunities when they come our way. If we are unprepared, we'll likely lose our chance to see and grasp these opportunities. As someone

once said, "Opportunities are never postponed; they are lost forever." The opportunity of a lifetime must be utilized in the lifetime of the opportunity.

Being prepared provides confidence. It's like the Chinese proverb, "When the student is ready, the teacher appears." When you're prepared, you know you'll be ready for the right opportunity. The danger in a lack of preparation is that we:

- Might remain blind to obvious opportunities

- Cannot mobilize quickly to take advantage of new opportunities

- Do not attract the right partners.

On the other hand, being prepared will pave the way to success. Success is simply the intersection of our preparation and our opportunity. When our preparation and our opportunities intersect, it can lead to great success.

There's no better example of the benefits of preparation than the Lewis & Clark expedition. Here were leaders facing unknown challenges, about to travel into a wild and often hostile environment, leaders who would never know what was around the next bend of the river.

The maps they had were extremely limited. Meriwether Lewis, who planned the expedition, had little information beyond his knowledge of the Ohio valley. To make matters worse, they couldn't send scouts beyond the Mississippi to gather advance information because of hostile French and Spanish armies. They couldn't plan because too much was out of their control. They had to be prepared. They had to be prepared for Indian attacks, they had to be prepared for hardship, and they had to be prepared in case they ran out of supplies.

> **Success is simply the intersection of our preparation and our opportunity.**

How did they transform what sounds like a suicide mission into a successful expedition, one that's still studied and celebrated 200 years later? Their success is credited to Lewis' preparation. "It was his meticulous preparations, not a grand sense of adventure, that ultimately ensured the expedition accomplished everything it had been tasked to do and more.[19"]

We can learn much from the leadership example of Lewis & Clark. Our journey may not be as historic, but our environment appears just as wild, doesn't it?

Can we afford to be any less prepared? How are we preparing ourselves for tomorrow as we climb the ladder to fulfill our destiny?

Teaching Points

- Planning is more difficult today because of the accelerated rate of change. That's why we must also be prepared.

- Planning involves methods used to achieve a specific result. Preparation is broader in its scope.

- We cannot assume that today's conditions will remain true tomorrow. We must be prepared for whatever comes our way.

- Leaders must be prepared on several levels:

  - Personal preparation includes the effect of our character, personality and hang-ups on future effectiveness.

  - Professional preparation involves remaining current in the area of our competency.

  - Relational preparation includes being aware of our chemistry and our ability to get along with all types of people.

  - Family preparation ensures that those we love are ready for whatever they will face.

  - Financial preparation involves arranging our income and expenses for the future.

  - Educational preparation includes reading, joining professional associations, consulting, and attending seminars so that we're current in the area in which we're working.

- Leaders who are adequately prepared will recognize new opportunities that come their way.

- Preparation guards us against becoming opportunistic.

- We pave the way to success by being prepared, as success is the intersection of preparation and opportunity.

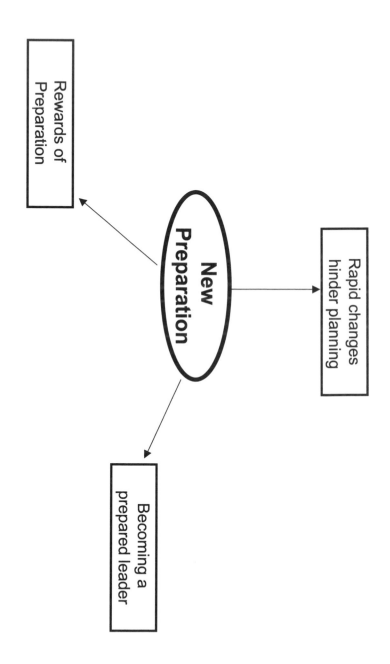

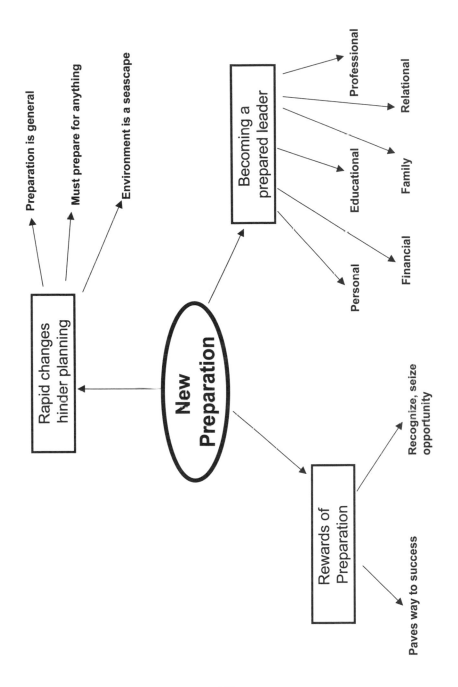

8

New Possibilities

The future is not the result of choices among
alternate paths offered in the present.
It is a place created – created first in the mind and the will;
created next in activity.

– Walt Disney, Founder of Disney Entertainment

ave you ever considered what makes your destiny so compelling?
Do you wonder exactly what it is that draws you onward? Have
you thought about why the music
that flows from your destiny attracts
you in the first place? Your destiny

> **...it's not just any future;**
> **it's *your* future.**

is attractive simply because it's a place that is overflowing with new
possibilities. It's a picture of a future that's filled with hope. And it's
not just any future; it's *your* future.

This book spent many pages describing the various challenges that
you'll encounter on your journey to fulfilling your destiny. While all
challenges are difficult, that's not the end of our story. The flip side is
that each time you respond to these challenges, you open the door to
new possibilities in your life and in the life of your organization.

As you climb the ladder to your destiny, you will be transformed. Don't
expect it to happen suddenly or even to be noticeable for some time.

Gradually, you will find that you've abandoned certain characteristics and traits in favor of newer, stronger ones. As a leader who has been transformed by your journey, you'll find yourself empowered to infuse your organization with this new life.

Traits of Transformed Leaders

Walt Disney described the future as, "*a place created – created first in the mind and the will; created next in activity.*" Our destiny, which is our future, is certainly a place that we create. Along the way, that journey transforms our attitudes, our thinking, and our commitments.

> **When unanticipated circumstances threaten, transformed leaders don't become rigid, demanding or controlling.**

I've found that leaders who are journeying toward their destinies exhibit the following characteristics:

- *Altered Attitudes:* The challenges you'll endure can produce a readiness to embrace change, an amazing adaptability to unexpected events, as well as a heart that's increasingly sensitive to others.

- *Transformed Thinking:* The situations that you'll encounter create an intellectual hunger that produces life-long learners, creative leaders, and an ease with a variety of technical issues.

- *Uncommon Commitments:* Leaders who are on the journey to their destiny also develop a passion for communicating and become skilled in building organizations engineered for the future.

Altered Attitudes

When you possess the trait of *change readiness*, you're much more inclined to willingly embrace change than to resist it. This simple attitude adjustment can produce vast gains. Consider how much more you could accomplish by being less controlling and more trusting of others. Think of the freedom that comes with being more aware of areas of your own thinking that need to change, as well as the obstacles that might be stopping you from making the necessary changes.

Change readiness also makes you more of a change advocate within your organization, someone who is able to promote change and help your people deal with the loss that they typically experience. When your organization becomes a change leader, it becomes a powerhouse that's able to move faster and get out in front of the pack with a can-do attitude.

When unanticipated circumstances threaten, transformed leaders don't become rigid, demanding or controlling. Their *adaptability* enables them not to be thrown by the unexpected. Instead, they fluidly travel with the flow of reality, making the necessary adjustments and

> **Their uncommon *sensitivity* makes them inclusive, rather than exclusive.**

redirecting to remain on course. Like trapeze artists, they've learned to maneuver courageously while trusting their instincts. They never seem to lose their forward movement or their momentum.

Transformed leaders don't roll over top of others while they're moving forward. Their uncommon *sensitivity* makes them inclusive, rather than exclusive. They don't play favorites. They've learned to celebrate cultural differences, as well as to honor the complementary force that

God deposited in both genders, capably harnessing this synergy in the workplace.

And this sensitivity extends even to the generation gap, which is no

> **Transformed leaders become lovers and advocates of life-long learning.**

longer about "sex, drugs and rock-n-roll;" these days the generation gap is about technology. Transformed leaders understand these issues and actively seek ways to extend their circle to welcome Baby Boomers, Baby Busters, Gen-Xers and the younger generation, known as Mosaics.

Transformed Thinking

With their curiosity stimulated by their encounters with increasingly challenging situations, these transformed leaders become lovers and advocates of *life-long learning*. They read widely, investigate outside of their own disciplines and probe others with insightful questions. They've become inquisitive explorers of the world around them and are always encouraging others to expand their own borders.

They've internalized Don Herold's statement, "It takes a lot of things to prove you are smart, but only one thing to prove that you are

> **"It takes a lot of things to prove you are smart, but only one thing to prove that you are ignorant."**

ignorant." They know that the phrase "knowledge is power" is truer today than ever before. They recognize that information is the new currency, and that this intellectual capital multiples

as they barter knowledge. You'll find them willingly sharing what they know. They've realized that innovation – in both speed and quality – is success, so they invest rather than hoard their currency.

They're the type of people who want to invest an hour each day in independent study. Why? Because they've realized that by scheduling time for study, even the average

> **...a vision without a strategy is only a dream...**

person can develop into an expert in their topic of choice in three to five years. They're excited by that possibility.

Ask them about their greatest pleasure in life and they'll talk about their love for accomplishing what others say cannot be done. You can see them applying this *creativity* in a number of critical areas:

- *Strategic thinking.* Transformed leaders know that hope is not a strategy. They know that a vision without a strategy is only a dream, and that they cannot be strategic if their efforts lack context. They'll praise a systems approach while simultaneously working hard at preventing those efforts from becoming overly complicated. They sagely recognize simplicity as competitive advantage. They may emphasize this point by telling you how the American space program spent millions to develop a pen that would write in zero gravity, while their former

  > **...recognize simplicity as competitive advantage.**

  Soviet competitors sent cosmonauts into space armed with pencils.

- *Genius thinking.* Despite their heavy schedules and massive workloads, they can quickly spot relationships and possibilities that others miss. That's what makes them leaders. They pioneer new ways of thinking and demonstrate their genius by seeing through things, as well as by seeing things through.

• *Oblique thinking.* Instead of being limited to an "either-or" mentality, transformed leaders have the capacity for "both-and" ideas. Their thoughts extend beyond vertical and horizontal limits to an angular reality. This orientation reveals to them a wealth of possibilities in what others refer to as "the impossible."

> **They can quickly spot relationships and possibilities that others miss.**

Transformed leaders don't need to be cured of technophobia. They're nothing like the executives of one prominent telecommunications firm who had to be forced to begin using computers. Instead, transformed leaders are characterized by *technophilia*, a willingness to embrace emerging technologies.

They realize the inherent *technical* aspects of even the most common organizational activities: how an usher greets you, how funds are raised, how a presentation is collated for an upcoming board meeting.

> **...transformed leaders are adept at *futuring*.**

They know that information is power, so they capitalize on information technology to send and receive newsletters, messages, and a wealth of other resources. Transformed church leaders who are cautioned about their technophilia gently remind their critics that the Reformation resulted from the church's use of the printing press. These transformed leaders are not shy about adopting business technology to measure their results, or to improve their effectiveness and efficiency.

Uncommon Commitments

Transformed leaders are intensely aware of the need to extend effective *communication* across generations, across cultures, as well as across this small globe that we inhabit.

They understand how even the most familiar terms can be misunderstood. They'll tell you that Baby Boomers interpret the question "why" as a disrespectful affront to authority, while the Gen-Xers posing

> **New possibilities become a natural, everyday occurrence**

the question are only seeking information and would appreciate an answer instead of an attitude.

They firmly believe that cross-cultural communication is not a course of study limited to those about to travel or work overseas. They see the world's residents daily in their own churches, organizations, and neighborhoods.

Most importantly, transformed leaders are adept at *futuring*. They forecast trends by scanning the horizon and can clearly envision future scenarios. While others are locked in the past or the present, they're actively creating the future through their present decisions and actions.

You'll find them wondering what the world will be like when the current crop of first graders are graduating from high school. They'll intentionally focus portions of their leadership meetings on the demographics, economic and competitive realities facing your organization five years from now.

And they'll capably equip their organization to create their own desired future. Like sherpa guides, they'll lead others up steep mountains to grasp

> **It doesn't mean that your rose-colored glasses magically enable you to declare every glass as "half full."**

a vision of the organization's future success. Once they've led their associates into this inspiring future state, they'll capably direct them in assembling the skills and perspectives that will transform this future into a present reality.

Unlocking a Wealth of Possibilities

Leaders who are willing to think and act in these new ways experience no shortage of new possibilities. In fact, new possibilities become a natural, everyday occurrence to them. Theirs is a future of limitless opportunity, boundless growth and unparalleled resources.

Focusing on new possibilities doesn't exempt you from experiencing your share of lean times and trying circumstances. It doesn't mean that your rose-colored glasses magically enable you to declare every glass as "half full."

When you focus on new possibilities in spite of your circumstance,

> **...new possibilities that can emerge from any and all situations.**

it signals that you're a leader who values a broadened and transformed perspective. It reveals that while you're climbing the ladder to your God-given destiny, you're keeping your eyes on the horizon. It means that from that altitude, you're quick to glimpse the sunrise and the first to perceive the new possibilities that can emerge from any and all situations.

Your new possibilities can become the milestone markers that light the road to your destiny. Each new possibility signals that you're moving ever closer to your desired destination.

Teaching Points

- Leaders who climb the ladder to their destiny will be transformed by their journey.

- They experience transformed attitudes, transformed thinking and transformed commitments.

- Altered attitudes:

  - *Change readiness* means you're inclined to willingly embrace change, an attitude that can produce vast gains.

  - An *adaptability* to unanticipated circumstances can keep you from being thrown off balance.

  - A *sensitivity* to others that celebrates differences, honors the complementary forces in both genders, enabling you to be inclusive rather than exclusive.

- Transformed thinking:

  - As a *life-long learner*, you recognize that information is the new currency, and that this intellectual capital multiples as knowledge is exchanged.

  - Applying *creativity* to accomplish what others see as impossible by thinking strategically, spotting possibilities that others miss, and not being limited by "either-or" thinking.

  - Characterized by *technophilia*, a willingness to embrace technology, using it to measure results and improve effectiveness.

- Uncommon commitments

  - Aware of the need to extend *communication* to generations, cultures and around the globe.

  - Adept at futuring, forecasting trends and future scenarios. Creating the future through today's decisions.

- Leaders who are willing to think and act in these ways experience no shortage of new possibilities.

- They recognize that new possibilities can emerge from any and all situations.

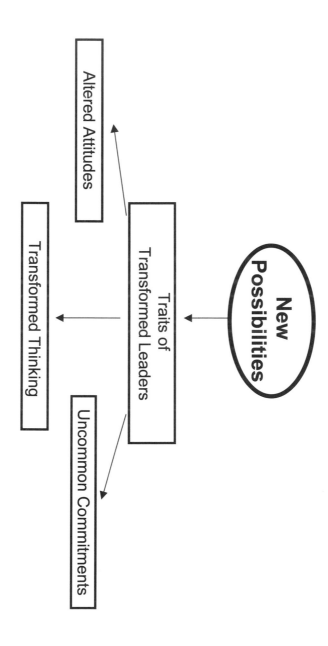

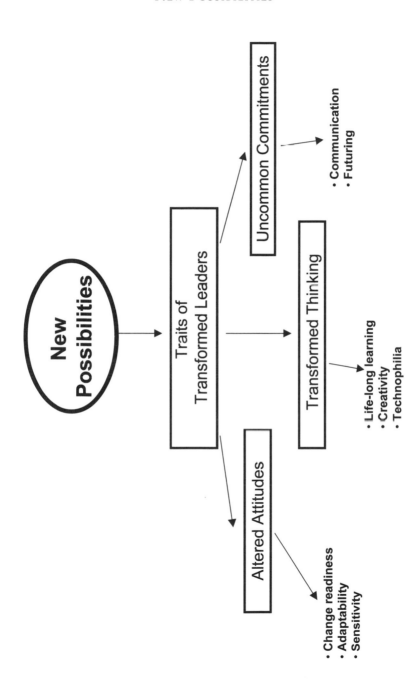

Bibliography

[1] Proverbs 23:7

[2] Genesis 1:26

[3] "How Jack Welch Runs GE," *Business Week*, June 8, 1998

[4] Proverbs 27:17

[5] "Herb Kelleher on the Record, Part 2," *Business Week*, Dec. 2003

[6] "The Painful Lives of Football Players," ABC News, http://abcnews.go.com/GMA/ESPNSports/story?id=1528986&CMP=OTC-RSSFeeds0312

[7] "Lessons in Leadership: The Education of Andy Grove," *Fortune*, Nov. 28, 2005

[8] "Even Healthy Churches Need to Change," *Leadership Journal*, Fall 2005

[9] "Can This Man Reprogram Microsoft?," *The New York Times*, Dec. 11, 2005

[10] "Level 5 Leadership: The Triumph of Humility and Fierce Resolve," *Harvard Business Review*, July-August 2005.

[11] "Managing for Business Effectiveness," *Harvard Business Review*, May-June 1963.

[12] Philippians 3:13

[13] "Inside the Mind of Jeff Bezos," *Fast Company*, Aug. 2004

[14] "The Softening of a Software Man," by John Heilemann, *New York*, Jan. 9, 2006

[15] "Mr. Superhero," *HBS Alumni Bulletin*, Vol. 81, No. 4, December 2005

[16] "Exit Strategies for Corporate Dropouts," *Fast Company*, March 2005

[17] Mary Ann Radmacher. Used by permission: www.maryanneradmacher.com

[18] Proverbs 16:9

[19] "Planning and Preparation," Lt. Col. Mark J. Reardon, Corps of Discovery, Center for Military History Online, http://www.army.mil/cmh-pg/LC/index.htm

About Dr. Samuel R. Chand

Who would have thought, when in 1973 *"student"* Samuel Chand was serving Beulah Heights Bible College as janitor, cook and dishwasher, that he would return in 1989 as *"President"* of the same college! Under his leadership it became the country's largest predominantly African-American Bible College.

Dr. Chand is a former Pastor, college President, Chancellor and now serves as President Emeritus of Beulah Heights University.

In this season of his life, Dr. Chand does one thing—Leadership. His singular vision for his life is to **Help Others Succeed.**

Dr. Chand develops leaders through:

- Leadership consultations
- Leadership resources—Books/CDs/DREAM RELEASER online coaching
- Leadership speaking

As a **Dream Releaser** he serves Pastors, ministries and businesses as a *Leadership Architect* and *Change Strategist*. Dr. Chand speaks regularly at leadership conferences, churches, corporations, ministerial conferences, seminars and other leadership development opportunities.

Dr. Chand...

- Consults with large churches and businesses on leadership and capacity enhancing issues
- Named in the top-30 global Leadership Gurus list

- Founder & President of Dream Releaser Coaching and Dream Releaser Publishing
- Conducts nationwide Leadership Conferences
- Serves on the board of EQUIP (Dr. John Maxwell's Ministry), equipping five million leaders world-wide
- Assists Bishop Eddie L. Long's leadership development
- Serves on the board of Beulah Heights University

Dr. Chand has authored and published 11 books.

FAILURE: *The Womb of Success*
FUTURING: *Leading your Church into Tomorrow*
WHO'S HOLDING YOUR LADDER?: *Selecting your Leaders—your most crucial decision*
WHO MOVED YOUR LADDER?: *Your Next Bold Move*
WHAT'S SHAKIN' YOUR LADDER?: *15 Challenges All Leaders Face*
LADDER*Shifts: New realities—Rapid change—Your destiny*
LADDER FOCUS: *Creating, Sustaining, and Enlarging Your BIG Picture*
PLANNING YOUR SUCCESSION: *Preparing for Your Future*
REChurch: *When Change is no Longer an Option*
MASTER LEADERS—*A collaborative book with George Barna*
WEATHERING THE STORM: *Leading in Uncertain Times*
CRACKING YOUR CHURCH'S CULTURE CODE: *Seven Keyes to Unleashing Vision & Inspiration*

Leaders are using Dr. Chand's books as handbooks world-wide in leadership development.

His educational background includes an honorary Doctor of Divinity from Heritage Bible College, a Master of Arts in

Biblical Counseling from Grace Theological Seminary, a Bachelor of Arts in Biblical Education from Beulah Heights University.

Dr. Chand shares his life and love with his wife Brenda, two daughters Rachel & Deborah, son-in-law Zack and grand-daughter Adeline.

Being raised in a Pastor's home in India has uniquely equipped Dr. Chand to share his passion—that of mentoring, developing and inspiring leaders to break all limits—in ministry and the marketplace.

For further information visit **www.samchand.com**

LEADERSHIP RESOURCES
BY SAMUEL R. CHAND

CRACKING YOUR CHURCH'S CULTURE CODE:

Seven Keys to Unleashing Vision & Inspiration

Strategies for transforming a toxic church culture. Why is it that the best strategic plans and good leadership often are not able to move churches in the desired direction? Sam Chand contends that toxic culture is to blame. Quite often, leaders don't sense the toxicity, but it poisons their relationships and derails their vision.

This work describes five easily identifiable categories of church culture (inspiring-accepting-stagnant-discouraging-toxic), with diagnostic descriptions in the book and a separate online assessment tool.

The reader will be able to identify strengths and needs of their church's culture, and then apply practical strategies (communication, control and authority, selection and placement of personnel, etc.) to make their church's culture more positive.

WEATHERING THE STORM:

Leading In Uncertain Times

Look around you. The world you live in isn't the world you grew up in. It is starkly different. Rapid advances in technology, innovative forms of communication, and globalization are a few reasons why the world you once knew is gone and will never return.

One thing on the planet remains the same - change. You live within this paradigm. Even harder, you lead others through this paradox. As a 21st century leader, you are called to weather the storm of change and lead others through uncertain times.

REChurch:

When Change Is No Longer An Option

If you are a pastor or a leader in your church, this book is a must-read. Delve into Re-Church and begin to understand the church's need to re-contemplate the vision using these approaches:

- Re-tooling
- Re-structuring
- Re-ordering
- Re-covering
- Re-connecting

PLANNING YOUR SUCCESSION:

Preparing For Your Future

In Planning Your Succession, you'll be encouraged and equipped to:

- Live by design, rather than default
- Assess the complex factors behind avoiding succession
- Move beyond considerations about filling vacancies and begin creating a sustainable future - for yourself and for your organization
- Apply a knowledge of what works and what doesn't
- Find inexpensive ways to develop a successor
- Explore your options if you're considering a transition
- Create a culture of succession at all levels in the organization
- See how incoming leaders can maximize their opportunities

LADDER FOCUS:

Creating, Sustaining, and Enlarging Your Big Picture

How to realize your organizational vision by illuminating the many necessary structural and procedural components. It includes easy-to-follow blend of principles, examples, and practical tips to equip you in ensuring the success of your organization.

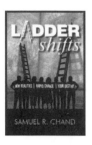

LADDER SHIFTS:

New Realities - Rapid Change - Your Destiny

No leader is immune to the shifting circumstances and events that can challenge or stymie their professional or organizational progress. Advance warning of these oncoming storms, together with adequate preparation, can mean the difference between disaster and success.

WHAT'S SHAKIN' YOUR LADDER?

15 Challenges All Leaders Face

Take an in-depth look at the common challenges that all leaders face, and benefit from practical advice on facing and overcoming the things that are blocking you from being the best you can be.

WHO MOVED YOUR LADDER?

Your Next Bold Move

Taking the next bold move is not easy—but you finally admit, "I have no choice. I have to jump!"

This book will equip you for that leap.

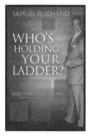

WHO'S HOLDING YOUR LADDER?

Leadership's Most Critical Decision—Selecting Your Leaders

Those around you, not you, the visionary, will determine your success.

WHO'S HOLDING YOUR LADDER?

(Spanish Edition)

This Version is entirely in Spanish. English Version is above.

FUTURING:

Leading Your Church into Tomorrow

The message will never change. But the methods to present the message can and must change to reach a realm of churchgoers.
Forty-four specific areas that are changing in the church today.

FAILURE:

The Womb of Success

- Failure is an event not a person
- Failure is never final
- Twenty leaders tell their stories

DEVELOPING A LEADERSHIP CULTURE

- Why do leaders do what they do?
- Why and when leaders make changes?
- Vision levels of people
- Contemporary leadership
- Why leaders fail
- Qualities of a successful leader

WHAT KEEPS PASTORS UP AT NIGHT

- Do my people get the vision?
- Are things getting done?
- How is the team working together?
- Do I have the team I need to get it done?

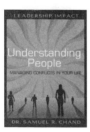

UNDERSTANDING PEOPLE:

Managing Conflicts in Your Ministry

- What conflict does
- High maintenance relationships
- Predictable times of conflict
- Levels of conflict
- Diffusing conflict
- Conflict resolution

CHANGE:

Leading Change Effectively

- Healthy confessions for those leading change
- Tradition and traditionalism
- Responding to seasons and times
- Levels of change
- Factors that facilitate or hinder change
- Steps for positive change
- Selling your idea
- Creating a team
- Personal challenges of the leader leading change

FORMATION OF A LEADER

Spiritual Formation
- Born to lead
- Security or sabotage

Skill Formation
- The day Moses became a leader

Strategic Formation
- Live the life you were meant to live
- Mentoring: How to invest your life in others

12 SUCCESS FACTORS FOR AN ORGANIZATION

- Handling Complexity
- Completion
- Lead and Manage People
- Executional Excellence

HOW DOES A LEADER THINK?

- Who am I?
- What is my address?
- What time is it?
- How will I know I'm successful?
- How will I deal with conflict?
- How do I maximize myself?

ORDER RESOURCES AT:

www.samchand.com

NOTES

NOTES

NOTES

NOTES

NOTES

NOTES

NOTES